STRANGER'S GUIDE

WHO WE ARE

BEFORE THERE WERE GUIDEBOOKS, 18th- and 19th-century authors wrote "stranger's guides," which were personal, eccentric and intimate portrayals of places. *Stranger's Guide* is a modern version of that idea—an award-winning publication that reveals the intricacies of locales across the globe, through both local and foreign eyes. Each print guide dives deep into a single location, featuring writers and photographers from those regions, on everything from sports and economics to fashion, politics and literature. Our work, which has garnered National Magazine Awards for General Excellence and for Photography, explores the power of place-based journalism to break down stereotypes and foster global citizenship.

PUBLISHER
Abby Rapoport

EDITOR IN CHIEF
Kira Brunner Don

CHIEF OPERATIONS OFFICER
Mike Kanin

MANAGING EDITOR
Kyla Kupferstein Torres

CREATIVE CONTENT EDITOR
Emily C. Skaftun

SPORTS/SENIOR EDITOR
Emily Nemens

SENIOR EDITORS
Alex Hannaford, Siddhartha Mahanta

LITERARY EDITOR
Joanna Yas

EDITOR AT LARGE
Courtney Desiree Morris

ASSOCIATE PUBLISHER
Ambia Elias

ASSOCIATE EDITOR
Cecilia Nowell

ASSOCIATE PHOTOGRAPHY EDITOR
Kike Arnal

ASSISTANT EDITORS
Annie Estes, Ajà Miller

COVER ILLUSTRATOR
Benjamin Frisch

WEB DESIGN
Blase Design

COPY EDITOR
Ian A. Walker

RESEARCH
Ethan Bien, Caren Gussoff Sumption

UKRAINE ISSUE EDITORIAL BOARD
Laada Bilaniuk, Michela Bowman, Dr. Vitaly Chernetsky, Boris Dralyuk, Misha Friedman, Michael Moser, Laura Secor, Haska Shyyan

CONTRIBUTING EDITORS
Kira Allmann, Joshua Beckman, Garnette Cadogan, Saneta deVuono-Powell, Kyle Haddad-Fonda, Stephanie Heimann, Roger D. Hodge, Joshua Jelly-Schapiro, Laleh Khadivi, Victor LaValle, Michelle Legro, Alexis C. Madrigal, John McMurtrie, Ayan Mittra, Martín Perna, Emily Raboteau, Betsy Reed, Laura Secor, Cassim Shepard, Lola Shoneyin, SA Smythe, Matthew Zapruder

SUBSCRIBE | strangersguide.com/subscribe
ADVERTISE | rapoport@strangersguide.com
RETAIL DISTRIBUTION
ambia@strangersguide.com
GET INVOLVED
facebook.com/strangersguidemag
@StrangersGuide
@StrangersGuide

Contributors

KRISTINA BERDYNSKYKH is an award-winning political journalist in Ukraine. The interviews that appear in this issue were first published in *Korrespondent* magazine in 2013–2014, in her *People* project about participants in Ukraine's Revolution of Dignity.

MISHA FRIEDMAN is a photographer who collaborates with leading international media and nonprofit organizations. A 2021 Pulitzer Prize finalist, his widely exhibited work has received numerous industry awards, including several Pictures of the Year (POYi).

ANASTACIA GALOUCHKA is a Belgian-Ukrainian who currently resides in Kyiv. Originally working as a lawyer in Belgium, she moved to Kyiv in 2019 to work as an expert in foreign policy and international law. During the 2022 war, she's been helping international journalists covering the war in Ukraine.

NATALIYA GUMENYUK is a Ukrainian journalist specializing in foreign affairs and conflict reporting, and author of *Lost Island: Tales from the Occupied Crimea*.

LILY HYDE is a writer and journalist based in Ukraine. She is the author of *Dream Land* and is working on a book about Crimea after 2014's annexation. She has written for the *The Guardian*, *The Times of London*, *POLITICO* and others.

DAVID KLION is an editor at *Jewish Currents* and has written for *The New York Times*, *The Nation*, *The New Republic*, *New York Magazine*, *Foreign Policy* and other publications.

VOLODYMYR RAFEENKO is a Ukrainian writer, novelist and poet. He is a three-time winner of the Russian Literary Prizes. In 2019, he published his first novel written in Ukrainian, *Mondegreen*.

ANDRII ROZANOV is a sports journalist and the editor of the boxing and martial arts section of the Ukrainian sports site Tribuna.com.

LAURA SECOR is a journalist whose work has appeared in *The New Yorker*, *The New York Times Magazine*, *Atlantic Monthly*, *New Republic* and other publications. She is the author, most recently, of *Children of Paradise: The Struggle for the Soul of Iran*.

HASKA SHYYAN is a Ukrainian author of prose and poetry, a translator, a culture manager and a producer of book trailers and podcasts. In 2019, Haska's second novel, *Behind Their Backs*, became the first Ukrainian novel to receive the European Union Prize for Literature.

ANASTASIA STANKO is a journalist and TV presenter. She is a member of the "Stop censorship" movement, made up of journalists and media organizations in Ukraine. In 2013, she co-founded the independent media channel, Hromadske, which is registered as a non-governmental organization, and where she currently is a member of the General Assembly.

OLEKSANDR TECHYNSKYI is a photographer and filmmaker. In 2014, he won Best Eastern European documentary at DOK Leipzig International Documentary Film Festival for his debut feature, "All Things Ablaze." Techynskyi has worked as TV 2's fixer in Ukraine during the 2022 war.

VASYLYNA VRUBLEVSKA is a fashion photographer based in Kyiv. Her work has appeared in *Vogue UA*, *Esquire Ukraine*, *Forbes Ukraine* and *Elle Ukraine*, among others. Her photos were published in *Ukrainian Black and White Photography XXI*.

Stranger's Guide [ISSN 2639-3638 (print) ISSN 2639-3646 (online)] entire contents copyrighted (c) 2022 is published quarterly by SG Studios, LLC. **Email:** info@strangersguide.com. **Customer Service:** [MAIL] P. O. Box 15007, Austin, TX 78761, [PHONE] (833) 848-5116. **Postmaster:** Send address changes to: P. O. Box 15007, Austin, TX 78761. **Subscriptions:** 1 yr $75. Back issues $22. Airmail, foreign, group and bulk rates available on request.

Stranger's Guide
UKRAINE

TOUR GUIDE — 4
SG's guide to Ukraine

FEATURES

Who We Are — 7
by Haska Shyyan
A meditation on Ukraine's tragedies and triumphs, joys and pains

Prisoners of War — 29
by Nataliya Gumenyuk
Mothers and children live together in prison during wartime

Party Revolution — 35
by Anastacia Galouchka
Rave culture breaks from the past to build something new

Conflicts of Interest — 45
by Laura Secor
Building a democratic media in Ukraine

Scenes from the War — 50
by Anastacia Stanko
The diary of a Ukrainian journalist

The Dark Side of the Moon — 63
by Volodymyr Rafeenko
In response to war, a writer abandons the Russian language

At the Limits of Nationalism — 75
by David Klion
Confronting Ukraine's past to imagine its future

The Broken Yoke — 97
by Andrii Rozanov
Emerging from boxing's "Soviet School"

PHOTOGRAPHY & ART

On the Road — 14
by Oleksandr Techynskyi

Malanka — 56
by Vasylyna Vrublevska

Ukrainian Romanticism — 82
by Misha Friedman

Iconic Ukraine — 104
Alight's Aid2Art program

FICTION

Knock Knock — 111
by Lily Hyde

FIRST PERSONS

Voices from the Maidan — 120
by Kristina Berdynskykh

TIMELINE — 42
LITERARY TOUR — 68
SOUND BITES — 128

KNOW BEFORE YOU GO **SUPERSTITIONS** *The dos and don'ts of good fortune [30]* **UKRAINE'S ODDEST MUSEUMS** *Sex, toilets & jellyfish [33]* **COOL KIDS** *Communist kitsch & hipster chic [37]* **EUROVISION** *Come for the music, stay for the politics [39]* **FALSE FRIENDS** *Russian & Ukrainian languages [66]* **LENINFALL** *The toppling of Soviet statues [77]* **CAFÉS** *Soviet v. anti-Soviet [78]* **THE HERMIT IN THE PALACE** *The people's squatter [81]* **#HEXPUTIN** *Witches of Instagram [100]* **CHERNOBYL** *Zone of Alienation [103]* **QUIZ:** *Spot the Ukrainian [114]* **GOT WHEAT?** *The bread basket of Europe [119]*

TOUR GUIDE

UKRAINE

UKRAINE IS THE LARGEST COUNTRY ENTIRELY IN EUROPE

UKRAINE HAS EUROPE'S LARGEST
- titanium reserves
- military force
- software development industry
- gas storage capacity

The only **ANTONOV AN-225** *ever built, the largest aircraft in the world, was destroyed in the Russian attack on Ukraine.*

As of August 2022, the title **Hero of Ukraine** had been conferred on:

- 652 SCIENTISTS, ATHLETES, ARTISTS, POLITICIANS & SOLDIERS
- 10 CITIES

1 river has been proposed for hero status for slowing Russian troops in 2022.

UKRAINIANS WEAR WEDDING RINGS ON THE RIGHT HAND.

When Ukrainians toast, they say "budmo," which means "let us be."

$400 USD: average monthly salary in Ukraine

The railways between Klevan and Orzhiv is wooded and known as the "Tunnel of Love." The trees were originally planted to cover up supply movements during the Cold War.

IN 1991, UKRAINE HELD THE THIRD-LARGEST NUCLEAR ARSENAL IN THE WORLD:

1,900 strategic warheads

176 intercontinental ballistic missiles (ICBMs)

44 strategic bombers

By 1996, Ukraine had returned all of its nuclear warheads to Russia in exchange for economic aid and security assurances.

DURING RUSSIA'S INVASION OF CRIMEA, A GROUP WITH THE MOTTO "DON'T GIVE IT TO A RUSSIAN" ENCOURAGED WOMEN TO BOYCOTT SEX WITH RUSSIANS.

51,493 STREETS & 987 CITIES & VILLAGES
with Soviet names were renamed in 2016.

In a 2022 poll, **76%** of Ukrainians supported renaming streets to be less Russian.

Ukraine has more than 2,500 wooden churches. The oldest was built in 1470.

Pornography is illegal, except for medical purposes.

THE WORLD'S LARGEST CROSSWORD PUZZLE IS ON THE SIDE OF AN APARTMENT BUILDING IN LVIV.

Each January, Christians leap into the icy Dnipro River to celebrate Epiphany.

KYIV'S COLORFUL NEIGHBORHOODS

COMFORT TOWN, Kyiv, features lego-like bright yellows, lime greens, blues, oranges & reds, contrasting with the surrounding Soviet-era housing.

Many of VOZDVIZHENKA's rainbow-colored houses stayed empty since construction in the 2000s. Locals call it the "MILLIONAIRES' GHOST TOWN."

DURING THE 1930S FAMINE THAT KILLED MILLIONS, SOME 2,500 UKRAINIANS WERE PROSECUTED FOR CANNIBALISM.

The recipe for Chicken Kiev was brought to Russia from Paris in the 1840s. It wasn't common in Kyiv until tourists began requesting it in the 1960s.

KYIV'S MUSEUM OF THE GREAT PATRIOTIC WAR HAS A PAIR OF NAZI GLOVES MADE OF HUMAN SKIN.

THE CITY OF BALAKLAVA IS KNOWN FOR ITS SEAFOOD, NOT WOOLEN MASKS.

OVER 2 DAYS IN 1941, MORE THAN 33,000 UKRAINIAN JEWS WERE KILLED AND BURIED IN THE BABYN YAR RAVINE. THE SITE WAS LATER USED AS A GARBAGE DUMP. IT TOOK 50 YEARS FOR AN INDEPENDENT UKRAINE TO PUBLICLY ACKNOWLEDGE THESE MURDERS WITH A MENORAH-SHAPED MONUMENT.

Every Rosh Hashanah, tens of thousands of Jews travel to Uman, burial place of Nachman of Breslov, founder of a Hasidic sect.

The world's longest musical instrument is a 27-foot-long Ukrainian trembita.

IN 2021, A FOLDING "POP-UP" SYNAGOGUE WAS UNVEILED AT THE SITE.

Kyiv Mayor Vitaly Klitschko was once the world heavyweight boxing champion.

SUNFLOWERS, UKRAINE'S NATIONAL FLOWER, REPRESENT PEACE.

It's believed that the first song sung in space was the Ukrainian "Watching the Sky," sung by cosmonaut Pavel Popovich.

Kyiv has the world's deepest subway station—Arsenalna, **346 FEET UNDERGROUND**

Ukrainian Dmitry Khaladzhi calls himself the world's strongest man. His stunts include carrying cows, horses and other livestock.

CHERNOBYL TOURISM:

$150-$500: cost of an excursion to Chernobyl before the latest conflict.

IN 2019, THE UKRAINIAN GOVERNMENT PAID BENEFITS TO **36,525 WIDOWS** OF MEN WHO SUFFERED AS A RESULT OF THE CHERNOBYL ACCIDENT.

Unmarked Russian soldiers in Crimea became known as "little green men."

RULES FOR VISITORS PROHIBIT:
- SHORTS, T-SHIRTS & SANDALS
- TAKING PHOTOS AT CHECKPOINTS
- POCKETING RADIOACTIVE "SOUVENIRS"
- EATING WILD BERRIES OR MUSHROOMS
- TOUCHING PLANTS OR BUILDINGS

Café Sign "Khutin Puylo," a play on the phrase "Dickhead Putin." Lviv. 2015. Photograph by Haska Shyyan.

Who We Are

A meditation on Ukraine's tragedies and triumphs, joys and pains

Haska Shyyan

The fact that you are holding this book in your hands, and even feel curiosity toward reading it, probably means you are interested in this massive land, situated somewhere between Europe and Russia. You probably still see it as terra incognita, and as part of mysterious Slavic space, with its intriguing and slightly wild soul. A cold territory inhabited by clones of Natalya Vodyanova where people speak a few similar languages, using Cyrillic to spell it all. Nevertheless, intuitively you feel that there must be something special and distinctive hiding around here. And also, you feel anxiety, wondering: how does a country that is at war live on a daily basis? Is it safe to land at its airports?

Or maybe not. Maybe you have traveled here enough times to learn that it actually can be pretty hot, is rather safe and yes, the trend for impressive eyebrows did recently expand across the region and female faces. And lumbersexual beards conquered the chins of young men. Maybe your knowledge of local specialities is even good enough to not get confused identifying the Ukrainian and Russian languages, hanging out with locals in one of chill and hip bars of Kyiv, which generously open their doors and summer terraces these days. In this case, you can be proud of the proficiency of a true linguist who cares about the letter "Ї," which we tenderly carry in the name of the country *(Ukraine is spelled Україна in Ukrainian— Ed.)*, as well as its capital. Although it does not necessarily make us naïve in our struggle for #KyivnotKiev *[a campaign calling to spell Ukraine's capital city as 'Kyiv' in English, according to Ukrainian phonetics (Київ), rather than 'Kiev' (Киев), in Russian phonetics—Ed.].* You will have quite a few confusing moments when opening maps of the country and cities. Sorry for that. But in the twentieth century, things were renamed so many times that it makes Chervonoarmyska, Bolshaya Vasilkovskaya, Krasnoarmeyskaya and Velyka Vasylkivska the same street, especially in the navigation inbuilt into the heads of taxi drivers. But anyway, be happy you have the luxury of avoiding listening

"Night Ambassadors" party. Bank Hotel, Lviv. 2018. Photograph by Haska Shyyan.

to political analysis "exclusively from behind the wheel." Even if you understand the language, pretend you don't—these experts "in everything in the world" can easily provoke you to run away.

And you better not.

There are many things to see around this country, and usually, you foreigners are even more passionate than us locals in exploring remote and hidden treasures. I will share my individual suggestions, feelings and memories, trying to balance between my personal few pages for *Lonely Planet Eastern Europe* and a personal friendly chat that should help to encourage, intrigue, seduce and invite. I won't go deeper into time than to glide over the Soviet era as, anyway, one young girl recently called it "ancient," giving me more confidence about my own life experience. Our history of the previous century is not a piece of cake, especially when it gets segmented into puzzling pieces of human stories with all their secrets and shades of emotions. Grandchildren often unite the radically different political views and reflections of their grandparents, mixing deep, painful traumas with sweet nostalgia. And the patchwork of these stories is, at the same time, such a strong celebration of our diversity and unity. Ukrainian culture is strongly associated with its ethnic and rustic origins (and rightfully so), but its urban landscape offers a wide spectrum: full of objects of admiration from the cute heritage of Austrian and Polish architects to Soviet empire style, functionalism and brutalism. Folk elements coexist successfully with the strong industrial and city culture, developed under various influences of more and less tolerant empires. Being an urban creature myself, I will take you on a tour around a few beloved cities, telling stories through the eyes of friends who helped me to discover a lot.

JULIA IN LVIV

Julia is just wonderful—I don't know how else I could start talking about her. She came over from Krakow, where she is doing her Erasmus. Who would not want to come from Barcelona to Krakow as Erasmus, really? Who would not go

Old ladies and kids. Levytskoho street, Lviv. 2016. Photograph by Haska Shyyan.

for a weekend from Krakow to Lviv! Or Lwow, as they keep calling it there *[in Poland—Ed.]*. Another confusion of letters and sounds. Julia was probably told that Lwow is almost like Krakow, but a bit quieter and cheaper. There's no easyJet connection from the UK, if you know what I mean. So, she grabbed her backpack and sent a CouchSurfing request to me and my sister, received almost immediate confirmation and left her 35-square-meters room in a huge, old shared apartment. Julia is an adventurous girl, so she decides to take a pedestrian crossing in Shehyni, packed with smugglers of cigarettes and vodka, competing with each other over the number of gold teeth, place in the queue and odors hidden in the layers of clothes they use as smuggling tools. After smiling to an indifferent border officer and getting through the labyrinthine path with the rest of the crowd, Julia gets on a marshrutka (a minibus), when it is already dark. *OMG*, thinks Julia, *where is this rusty yellow bus, floating like a submarine in the cold black October air, going to take me?* The soundtrack is far from recognizable Beatles melodies, the driver is crossing himself when traveling by every church and statue of the Holy Virgin—the only enlightened islands…ah, okay, the petrol stations too…but there are more Holy Virgins. Front window decorations consisting of tons of weird stuff, from religious items to naked girls and fluffy toys, make road visibility even worse. The driver crosses himself again. Is he so scared to drive here? His face reflects the opposite—a peaceful experience is resting in his wrinkles. Even when the bus jumps over a new pothole whose location he does not yet know by heart. He does swear. Julia recognizes the Polish word "kurwa" in a longer list of unknown expressive obscenities. But his heavily suntanned forehead, his plump red cheeks, his tired gaze stay almost frozen. Even his lips don't really move—the words come from the depths of his heart—only his strong hands, with stains of black soil and oil, twist the wheel harshly. The metal makes the sound of a dog being beaten, and some passengers sigh. *Where is it going to take me?*—Julia asks almost out loud. And instinctively replies to herself: *C'mon Julia, it should be fine and maybe even fun.* Ha ha, she still does not know my phone has only one percent battery life and a risk of not being heard in a loud bar. It is Friday night, after all. Although, my life in Lviv back then was an endless Friday night.

Julia arrives at the train station at midnight, like Cinderella on a yellow pumpkin, except that this vehicle does not have more potential to degrade. The building is rather gorgeous; it seems like it is recognizable from one of the movies she watched recently. The city is more generous with the lights than countryside roads are. My phone is charged again, as not so many bars offer drinks after 11 p.m. This place is not as wild as you sometimes would want it to be, Julia. You won't meet too many loud gangs hanging out 'til dawn. Instead, it offers the coziness of a hot meal, an uncorked bottle of wine and a soft sofa to sleep on. We chat for a few hours, and Julia becomes almost like our sister very quickly, so the next day, we decide to show her real Lviv, with all the layers of epochs, skipping the ticks in the boxes of well-promoted touristy "musts."

We start in one of the coffee places that could easily be called dodgy, right behind the corner of the once-luxury George Hotel. The sculptures on the façade turn their butts and open their breasts to the cold October sun. The air is crispy, fresh and the light is golden orange. We roll our cigarettes outside; they burn our lips together with the shot of strong black liquid from an old-school machine. Men in their late 50s inhabit the place, with their elegant gray hair, torn violin cases and flutes under their arms. They have their morning cognac and try to flirt with us in a manner that's as vintage as their faded coats. One of them even makes it to kiss Julia's hand. And cheek. Her face blushes. He bows, like on the stage of an opera house, grabs aged sheet music and leaves to teach a new generation of orchestra players at the conservatory across the street. We go ahead to Rynok Square—yes, it is a "must," but we still don't skip it; we're just going to watch it from different angles. A corner location is perfect for that. In a small, authentic Greek tavern—the owner settled down here for a few years and decided to share his cooking skills with locals. We grab some pitas and sit outside, as we're offered a secret glass of ouzo as a compliment. The smell of anise, along with the sun which shares the last warmth of the year, takes us south. Soon, everything is going to get humid and gray, and in a year or two, most of the places we visit today will no longer exist, replaced by trendier ones. Such are the lively dynamics of cities like Krakow, but cheaper. Low-cost flights will soon land in a tiny and homey airport. Some locals will complain, some will be happy, but for now, Julia and the rest of us just move our chairs, meter by meter, avoiding the shadow. The ancient stones around have their own way of measuring time. One more century, with all its historical turbulence, is nothing for them. "They've seen Austro-Hungary, Poland, the USSR and, finally, Ukraine, and they will still find a little hole between the bricks to hide a little memory of Julia."

Before sunset, we walk up the hill to see the city from the top. It is golden with all its churches and autumn parks. Coming back through proletarian industrial neighborhoods, which after the last wave of gentrification don't look like such a bad place to live, we stop at the brand-new playground and get on the swing. "I love this city!" says Julia. And this city loves her.

ERDEM IN KYIV

Erdem lands in Boryspil Airport and is happy not to look for a connecting flight and to discover his guitar was not damaged by Turkish Airlines. He has heard that this country is full of opportunities and wants to try outsourcing for IT, but also maybe cracking a deal with a small manufacturer of funky, colorful socks. Erdem is full of ideas and hopes, and after registering a LLC and getting a residence permit, his Dutch boyfriend is going to join him to settle down. I help him with bureaucratic practicalities—people all around the world find paperwork challenging, scary or even repulsive. The hot air outside can easily compete with temperatures in Istanbul, so it's hard to believe that in six months time a warm parka will be necessary. A taxi takes Erdem across the bridge over the River Dnipro, whose waters are calm and magnificent. The car smells like cheap perfume, the music is a bit strange and the driver can not keep himself from pronouncing the word "devochki—girls" in a context Erdem does not understand, but guesses about. Nevertheless, he decides not to go into the details of his private life too much as he intuitively feels that taxi drivers all over the world can be very judgmental.

We meet at the hotel lobby, which is inhabited by the bright and young. Colorful hair (magenta, lemon, teal), baggy clothes, piercing and tattoos.

> **THEY HAVE THEIR MORNING COGNAC AND TRY TO FLIRT WITH US IN A MANNER THAT'S AS VINTAGE AS THEIR FADED COATS.**

Independence Day. Ivan Franko Park Lviv. 2015. Photograph by Haska Shyyan.

Hipster culture blossoms here, on the terrace overviewing the roofs of Podil—a neighborhood that makes Kyiv feel like New Berlin more than others.

In the 2010s, this city was full of hardly digestible, tacky glamor, but underground night clubs hosting the best DJs, and not pretentious bars and cafés, take it further and further away from nouveau-riche bandit aesthetics, turning the place into a very vibe-filled location.

After discussing boring logistics and convincing Erdem that everything is doable without bribery, we start to research the funky sock market and discover that one of the brands designed in Lviv, close to the Polish border, is manufactured a few kilometers from the front line in Luhansk Region. Colorful threads 1,500 kilometers long connect people in the West and East and are also a reminder that we are a country at war. Erdem starts to ask. I try to explain. He listens.

"Annexation, invasion, separatism, occupation, IDPs—words that hardly correlate with the joyful crowd of youngsters chilling on the grass and kids splashing at the fountains, with the street food by the river and the white yachts floating back and forth."

Erdem does not even know that communist monuments have been demolished within the last few years—I tell him this, too. He wonders why. Bathing in orange sunset, boys are playing football and girls are skipping in the synagogue yard, all dressed traditionally. Their fathers discuss some important issues after the service. Teenagers cosplaying as unicorns pass by; nicely groomed puppies bark at the street dogs and then sniff each other, wagging their tails.

I decide to share an interesting experience with Erdem, to make him fully understand if this city is made for him (or he is made for it).

We go to visit a cemetery. Not that I think it is the first place to check if you have chemistry with the city, but that's where the play of immersive theater starts. I am not sure I would end up here on a different occasion, but that's what is so intriguing about it. Graves are located in the middle of the city, behind the hospital built in the Soviet era. The disturbing quietness of the place is expected, but embarrassing at the same time. There is a tombstone in the shape of a football field, and Erdem picks it to start the journey, according to the instructions in the headphones. A group of 30 people becomes both disconnected and connected at the same time. This brave experiment takes us to an underground pedestrian crossing full of kiosks selling meat, flowers, lingerie and even manicures. We are clapping the crowd entering the metro—it's a part of the game. *Beep-beep.* I pay with my phone to enter the station, increasing the rating of Ukraine as a contactless country. Couples are kissing on the escalators, and our group makes funny moves imitating ballet dancers. A Black guy with dreadlocks hops on the train, and we follow him, feeling so detached and so integrated in this flow of life while still wearing our headphones. Getting back up to the city's surface, we find ourselves protesting in front of the administrative building and dancing at the entrance of a luxury department store. We end up on the rooftop, watching the central avenue of Khreshchatyk as a toy model full of tiny cars and people.

After the 12 kilometer walk is over, we are starving—the choice of seafood in the food court makes us greedy, and we cannot stop picking the shrimp and sashimi for takeaway.

Designer dresses are waving at us almost as humans: black with pink fish pattern, lemon yellow with blue unicorns; perfumes and makeup collections are trying to convince us of their importance. We run away empty-handed.

Full of sticky pleasures, the summer night leaks to the frying pan of the streets like pancake batter. We are eating peaches and raspberries while sitting on a bench. The city does not fall asleep, and we stay up till dawn too, changing places and company, getting to the dance floor at the abandoned factory, walking a new pedestrian bridge with a stunning view of endless perspective. "My mother taught me to do exercises for my eyesight," Erdem says, concentrating on the detail very close and very distant. "I do it every morning. I will do it here. After jogging." "Well, wait for winter to come, Erdem, and let's see where your ophthalmological meditation is going to take you," I reply. And we both laugh. He definitely wants to stay. I recommend a handy application to order drinking water—they deliver within an hour. "Don't drink from the tap, Erdem; it tastes like just it's been pumped from the river! For everything else, this city is a great home!"

STEFANIA AND THREE OTHER GIRLS IN ODESA

What can be better than a night train to Odesa in early September?

Our compartment is filled with girlish gossip and careless joy. We are lying in our bunks covered with crisp linens, listening to the wheels on the track, drinking ritual tea in traditional thick glasses with metal holders and exercising our wit about the most important things in the world. That is what the mood of the next three days is going to be.

Arriving at 6 a.m., after a two-hour power nap, I am still able to think the morning is glorious and assume that it would be not so bad to try and catch more of those, finally accepting the fact that there is a point in starting the day before noon.

We're heading straight for the coastline, grabbing a few bottles of champagne on the way.

The beginning of the school year vacuumed up noisy kids and clucky mothers with lunchboxes from the beaches. Only a few aged, sun-tanned sardines and seals were left here and there. The warm saltiness and peaceful sand are almost just for us. Sweet corn and shrimp vendors pass by, completing our perfect picnic, which attracts a flock of hyperactive sparrows and a few lazy, mean seagulls. With the help of the sea breeze, our skin gets brown very quickly and we feel like queens of the beach until one of us notices the diva lying on the chaise longue and putting pieces of watermelon into her mouth piece by piece. She is in her early 70s, at least. Fit and dark brown, with makeup and hair done in the style of the 1980s, she's obviously spent every single day of the previous 20 summers here, in this bearable Odessness of being. She stretches, stands up and walks, full of grace, and then starts to run straight to the water, taking a long swim that wakes up the desire for competition in us. The salty water tickles our skin and leaves white straps all over when we let it dry, running along the tiny waves of the tide.

"I know what we're going to do in the evening!" Stefania says. "Let's sit on the promenade and read the prints on people's T-shirts!"

We sign up for the game.

"Let's meet in Paris!" insist the letters in glitters on the bosom of babushka. "BALI" her old friend silently declares in a large Panama hat.

It starts to rain.

The girl in the headphones does not care, she walks on by, singing.

"Let's go to the Seventh Kilometre market tomorrow and buy ourselves T-shirts with the word 'ODESA' emblazoned on them," Stefania suggests. "Not really sure they sell them there," we reply in chorus.

The evening city gazes around like a woman who has sent her man sailing.

...

I could go on and on.

Like a car trip to Berdychiv with a French friend of mine, for example, just because Honoré de Balzac got married there. Or the Christmas adventure of a Mexican guy in Ivano-Frankivsk—the winter story is missing in this collection.

One can say that this patchwork of glimpses does not tell any story. Where is the tradition? Where is the culture, the national spirit? But these flashes are true and the real quintessence of all that. The diversity of daily life, mixture of languages, unity of generations, layers of epochs.

Summer night. Derybasivska street, Odesa. 2020 Photograph by Haska Shyyan.

I've met so many coming here to discover.

To join the crowds of jazz, literature, theater, film festivals.

Trying to understand why people here can be insulted when you say The Ukraine, or ask if Russian and Ukrainian are actually different languages.

All these friendships keep helping me to explore my own country better, as many of them know it better than I do.

They are the ones going to Uman for a Jewish pilgrimage or to Pereyaslav-Khmelnytsky to see the parachute of Yuri Gagarin exhibited in the Museum of Space, located in an old church or traveling to Lutsk Soviet Bus Station as an example of unique architecture (oh yeah, who would have thought!)

I've met a Japanese man who was only interested in ticking off one box: taking a picture of the Tunnel of Love for his Instagram (good thing mosquitos are not visible in the photos).

A Mongolian man who traveled around the world for two years, survived in Africa and decided to challenge the Carpathian Mountains in winter. February is not the best time to enjoy the region, especially if you are not the biggest fan of depression caused by sun deprivation.

There was an Irish biker who went as far as Kinburn Spit, a wild and remote national park by the sea.

I've seen a lot of adoration for the Ukrainian countryside in the eyes of travelers and a willingness to help with the introduction of garbage recycling.

I've met those who followed the fall of the Lenin statues under the law of decommunization, and visited Corruption Park, helping us to heal the traumas of the past and uncover the shameful present.

All of them tried to understand our revolutions and wars, share our tragedies and triumphs, our pains and sorrows, our joys and victories.

They made me look at our country through a magnifying glass, watching its precious little lives. Human pearls and diamonds, iron nails and sponges. You are welcome to join them and help us to discover ourselves even better! ✺

On the Road
Oleksandr Techynskyi

WHEN THE RUSSIANS INVADED, Oleksandr Techynskyi, a documentary filmmaker, quickly moved his wife and two teenage daughters out of the country. He then took a job helping a foreign TV crew cover the war. Where he once spent his days making lyrical films and documentaries, he now spends endless hours crisscrossing the country in a car full of foreign journalists. With his own work on hold and his family away, he began snapping photos out of the car window.

Techynskyi's photos are reminiscent of stills from movies. "This is an apocalyptic noir that shows our present—heavy leaden clouds and ruined homes," he says. "The car passes people resembling zombies with empty eyes." Stopping among these ruined landscapes will inevitably lead to the death of the protagonist. "He himself will turn into a zombie and he will also wander the mazes of war-torn cities," says Techynskyi, who has no breaks from the war.

"I clearly remember only the endless road," he says. "Now when I have an unexpected weekend, I come home. There is no one there. My wife and children have been evacuated. I wander around the house and can't find a place. I can't sleep. It is a black hole. Here, the nausea is even stronger."

Rather than remaining at home, he asks for yet another assignment, escorting a fresh crew of TV journalists. "I want to go back. At least I feel alive there."

Prisoners of War

How conflict changed life for children living with their incarcerated mothers in Ukraine

Nataliya Gumenyuk

On the back seat of Iryna Bobrova's car is a copy of George Orwell's *1984*. She gives the novel to colleagues she thinks might be prone to Russian propaganda.

Bobrova is employed at a women's prison in central Ukraine that, for security reasons, cannot be named. She has worked there for 25 years, serving as its director for the past 15 years. She sees the worst of people at the prison, she says. But also the best. She admires how people can aspire to be good under ethical leadership. She also tells prisoners she is their mirror: "If they are good, I'll show my best," she says. "If they are tough, they see I can be tough as well."

The prison is one of five Ukrainian penitentiaries where children are allowed to stay with their mothers until age 3. Fifteen children live there now—the maximum the facility can accommodate. In all, 300 women are serving time in the prison. In Ukraine, most women charged with crimes must pay fines or serve probation. Prison sentences for women are handed down only for repeat offenders or serious crimes, including murder, robbery, child pornography and corruption.

Running a prison during wartime has made Bobrova rethink her priorities. Especially when the fighting has been a few hundred miles away—not that far in a time of long-range missiles.

"In the beginning, I was scared," she says. "We were instructed that in case of emergency, an administration might make independent decisions on how to act. We gathered in a kind of a general headquarters. We discussed all the options: occupation, armed resilience—though we do not have many arms here. At some point, I even thought, we can make a hole in the fence and let the mothers escape. We considered that the employees might temporarily take the babies. At the same time, we also have a very good bomb shelter, so I suggested the employees live here with the families, if needed."

A women's prison. Chernihiv. 2018. Photograph by Misha Friedman. This essay was produced in partnership with Impact Justice.

SUPERSTITIONS

Never eat from a knife, or you will become an angry person (or just cut your mouth by accident).

IT'S GOOD LUCK TO SIT BETWEEN TWO PEOPLE WITH THE SAME NAME.

40th anniversaries are not celebrated because the number 40 is associated with death. In the Eastern Orthodox church, it's believed that souls wrestle with demons for 40 days before finding their eternal resting place, and a memorial is held on that day.

Never give an even number of flowers, except at a funeral.

At tables, single people who sit at the corner will never marry.

If you step on someone's foot, ask them to step on yours or you will soon be on bad terms with each other.

Never pass anything across the doorstep or sit on it, lest you disturb the ancestors whose ashes, in ancient times, would have been buried underneath.

NEVER TAKE THE GARBAGE OUT AFTER SUNSET
or you will be surrounded by bad rumors and suspicions of malintent. It's also a good way to allow evil spirits into the house, who will then stay overnight.

A child can be cursed through a photo, so many parents forego posting pictures online. Others blur or put stickers over their babies' faces.

Wear safety pins to protect against curses and the evil eye. Safety pins absorb the negative energy of someone attempting to harm you—an iron pin will rust and a copper one will darken.

Don't whistle inside a home.
People once believed that whistling summoned evil spirits who would steal all present and future fortune. You shouldn't have time to whistle while working hard, and prosperity comes only through hard work.

Prisoners and employees alike were most anxious during the first month of the war. Citizens and institutions were advised by the government not to turn on lights in the evening, so as not to be visible to Russian forces. Prisons in Ukraine are often located in industrial zones, areas often targeted during shelling.

Bobrova's concerns were well founded. Two out of five women's prisons similar to this one were attacked during the first month of the war. One of them is near a major steel plant in Mariupol, the southern port city that was heavily bombed in the spring of 2022. In March, many civilians were trying to flee the city despite Russia's unwillingness to provide a green corridor for their safety. Power stations were deliberately bombed by the Russian army to make the city unlivable. Without electricity, the water supply can't work properly. Ukrainian authorities said they couldn't expect Moscow to follow the basic rules of war. Prisoners at the Mariupol prison became unruly and were fighting each other, the head of that facility told Bobrova.

In Melitopol, in southeastern Ukraine, which was occupied during the first days of the war, Russian occupiers forced local officials to shift allegiances. The head of the local prison fled town.

Several months into the war, Bobrova feels confident that her prison is less at risk of a siege. Should there be a siege, she says, there is enough food and resources to survive for at least half a year.

Bobrova is an attractive, middle-aged woman who dresses elegantly. She speaks with the steely authority that comes with her job. There were tears in her eyes, however, when she told me about buying meat for the prisoners' children at a local supermarket. She felt bad for depleting so much of the store's supply, and when she explained this to other customers in line, an elderly woman approached her and handed her 200 hryvnia (roughly $5).

The prison building where mothers live with their children is lined with images from cartoons. It's a tidy and colorful space that looks a bit like a nursery or children's dormitory. But the women in it are dressed in black; when they go outside, they must wear headscarves or hats.

Tetyana Yaroshenko, the director of what is called the Kids' House, began working at the facility in 1998. She retired in 2020, in her mid-40s, but recently returned. When we enter the building, it's clear that Yaroshenko knows every child well. She mentions one who started to walk a few days ago. While we're chatting with the prisoners, I spot a female guard who takes a minute to dress a curly-haired boy in a T-shirt that reads "Daddy's son." Ironically, most of the children have single mothers.

Bobrova and Yaroshenko explain that men rarely stay with convicts. The prison has numerous rooms for meetings, and visitors are allowed to come for three days. But the rooms are

A women's prison. Chernihiv. 2018. Photograph by Misha Friedman.

often empty. It's usually the prisoners' mothers, and their other children, who visit.

When Bobrova was developing a system for the prison, she wanted to model it after her own experience as a mother. She believes young mothers should have at least some breaks and can't stay near their babies 24 hours a day, seven days a week. And so she developed a sort of kindergarten where nannies look after the youngest children at times.

Bobrova and Yaroshenko see their mission as bringing out the "maternal instinct" in the prisoners. She does not idealize them, she says, insisting that there are good and bad ones. Many of them have problems with drugs, come from abusive families or are gang members.

"If somebody looks like a perfect mother in detention, it can't be the case in freedom," she says. "This year, I lived through major disappointment. There was a girl here, sentenced for murder, but an extremely kind and good mother. She explained her crimes by systematic abuse, in her family, then in the husband's family. She had the most beautiful boy, whom we all admired. If the mother remains in prison, the child could be given to relatives or temporarily adopted. Yet if the mother would be released in less than a year, after the kid turns three, there is a chance he stays with the mother until the end of the term. We did everything possible in this case to request her earlier release," Bobrova says with regret. Yet as soon as the girl was freed, she returned to her previous

A women's prison. Odesa. 2018. Photograph by Misha Friedman.

life. The administration saw the mother asking for money on Facebook and the boy looking neglected. Bobrova wondered: would it have been better if the mother had stayed longer and the child had been given to a foster family? There are many good parents who return to a normal life, she notes, yet if they have no place to turn to, they will likely commit crimes again.

Bobrova and Yaroshenko strongly defend the system that allows mothers to be with their children when they are young, given that conditions for the kids are often worse on the outside. And Bobrova is proud of the work that she has undertaken to refurbish and decorate the cells.

In the canteen, she says, jokingly, "You should have seen it before. People would say it looked like 'a prison.' Now, it's just 'an institution.'" She adds, "When people are deprived of basic things like food and comfort, they think just about that imminent need—they won't reconsider what they did or why they're serving their term. That's why a certain level of dignity should be maintained—mental space to reflect [on] the past."

As it happens, I visited the prison during the biggest air raid in Ukraine since the start of the invasion. The country, including the capital of Kyiv, was targeted with scores of missiles, at least half of which were shot down by air defense forces.

It was the first time during the war when prisoners did not complain that they needed to stay in the bomb shelter for more than five hours.

"In the very beginning," Bobrova says, "there was a person who said, 'it's your war, the war is there behind the fence—we have nothing to do with it.'"

Bobrova likes to say that her prison is a small projection of the state. If one looks at the individual destinies of the prisoners, it does reflect many Ukrainian tragedies that have taken place since the start of the full-scale Russian invasion.

Nadia (names of prisoners have been changed) is from Northern Saltivka, one of the most destroyed neighborhoods of Kharkiv—the second-largest city in Ukraine that has been heavily shelled since the first day of invasion. Nadia's oldest daughter, who is 19, was just meters away from an explosion. While cradling her son in her hands, Nadia speaks of her husband, who from March until September lived under the Russian occupation in a village that had no phone service.

Olha, who is serving an eight-year sentence, gave birth to a son in detention in January 2022. She is from a village in the southern Mykolaiv region; it's not occupied but is close to the frontline. Her husband works in Kremenchuk, an otherwise peaceful town in central Ukraine where a rocket destroyed a shopping mall on June 27, killing more than 20 people.

One prisoner, Vira, approached me to ask if I knew anything about the prison in Mariupol. She had been incarcerated there before being evacuated to Western Ukraine, then taken to the prison. She has no idea what happened to her former companions.

Svitlana comes from occupied Melitopol. Her five-year-old daughter was in a boarding school there, and there are rumors that it was relocated. Svitlana is at a loss as to how she can get any news about her daughter.

The colony's headmaster tells a story of a woman who nearly collapsed upon finding out that her father, who raised three of her kids, died in the conflict zone. Fortunately, it was only a rumor, and he was still alive.

Alla tells of how when she was brought to the prison from a detention center in Bakhmut region, shells were falling around her van.

Yulia comes to me to ask for help in finding her son. He joined the army and is now considered a missing person. "I am in touch with my husband," she says, "and as soon as I ask about him, my husband tries to change the topic. My elder son is in prison in another town, the youngest is too small, but I will be released in four months. And when I am free, I'll go search for him." Yulia says this with a sad smile.

Daria, who is 20, believes that her boyfriend, who is 22, is a Russian prisoner of war. He had disappeared since the last time they spoke, in February. Daria calls his mother once a week, concerned that she is being fooled by people who demand money in return for her son.

Bobrova says the prisoners want the same things: to be released, to see their children. But while talking with a group of them, one says, "Now, it's not usual. Yes, I was always worried for my family, I wanted to talk to kids—but nothing like now." ❋

UKRAINE'S ODDEST MUSEUMS

MUSEUM OF THE TOILETTE HISTORY, KYIV

Received the Guinness World Record for "largest collection of souvenir toilets in the world" in 2015, with

524 TOILETS

Jellyfish Museum, Kyiv

Because of the short life cycle of jellyfish, the collection is updated at least 3 times a year.

Pysanka Easter Egg Museum, Kolomyia

- Part of the building is a 13-meter-tall Easter egg.
- Contains 12,000+ decorated eggs from Ukraine and around the world.

MUSEUM OF SEXUAL CULTURES OF THE WORLD, KHARKIV

Must be 18+ to fully experience

MUSEUM OF UNNECESSARY THINGS, KYIV

- Since 1943, this recycling plant has curated interesting discarded objects for display.
- Over 1,000,000 items have passed through: gramophones, typewriters, a prototype shaving machine, boots and hand grenades.

State Museum of Toys, Kyiv

Founded by the USSR in 1933, the museum houses 15,000 toys selected by the People's Commissariats of Education.

NICOLAI SYADRISTY'S MICRO MINIATURE MUSEUM, KYIV

Microscopes are required to view Syadristy's art: a 3.5mm gold frigate or a tray with wine bottle and glasses atop a grain of salt. Syadristy also wrote a book called *Is It Difficult to Shoe a Flea?*

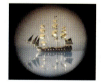

Party Revolution

Rave culture breaks from the past to build something new

Anastacia Galouchka

Summer 2019. It's 3 a.m., and I am lying in a hammock in the middle of the woods, just north of Kyiv. The moon and starlight barely stream down through the dense canopy of trees. But an area some 100 meters away from me pulses from the glow of blue and red flashing laser lights and lanterns strung here and there. There, a crowd gathers around a stage, about 60 square meters in size, roaring to a DJ's feral music. The revels won't end any time soon: Raves like this often go all night, lasting well into the following afternoon. While I find myself needing a breather, rest couldn't be further from the minds of the ravers. They stamp their feet into the ground in a frenzy, the reverberations rippling across the forest bed. I close my eyes, drinking it all in.

In 1986, my parents, a Russian-Tatar woman and a Ukrainian man, met in Perm, Russia, and fell in love. Seeking a better life for themselves and their one-year old son, they settled together in Antwerp, Belgium; in 1993, they had me. Like in many immigrant families, my parents struggled to make ends meet. They pushed us to excel academically to fulfill the dreams they'd had when they first moved abroad. In Leuven, I enrolled in law school. From there, the rest of my life seemed predestined: work at the same firm for 40 years; buy a big villa; pay off a never-ending mortgage; retire without having ever actually lived. I realized I wouldn't be any good at it. For years, I had traveled back and forth to Ukraine, attempting to connect with my roots. A cloud of uncertainty hung over the country, due to deep-rooted corruption, the frozen conflict in the east and constant economic struggles. A life of stability there felt impossible. Yet the chaos also offered more variety—excitement, even. In Ukraine, I could reinvent myself and contribute to its democratic reforms. In January 2019, two years after finishing law school, I moved to Kyiv to work at a local NGO, focused on democratic development through international cooperation.

Five months later, my eclectic new collection of friends—designers, doctors, musicians, IT workers and journalists—

Brave! Factory Festival. Kyiv. 2021. Photograph by Gueorgui Pinkhassov/Magnum.

invited me for what they thought would be a perfect introduction to the real Kyiv. Rhythm Büro, a group of local party organizers founded in 2015, had announced its third annual Natura rave, an event meant to unite its core audience of alternative-minded creative people and veteran ravers with new, less-established artists. The rave scene here bears some similarities to its Western counterpart: dark rooms, techno music and crazy leather outfits. But it goes beyond that. It's less focused on dress code, and more on self-expression and comfort.

We gathered at my friend's apartment near Klovs'ka to find out where we were headed: Rhythm Büro would only reveal the location of the event via text message 24 hours in advance. Finally, the coordinates came through: a place deep in the woods, about 30 kilometers north of Kyiv. On that sunny afternoon in June, we piled into a taxi and headed into the unknown. Upon arrival, we pulled over by the side of the road and proceeded on foot down a dirt path that led us deeper into the forest. We followed the sound of music and loud chatter. On a long stretch of road leading into the woods, we found over 2,000 people wandering through the forest, toward the music, ready to dance.

For me, Ukraine had always been the land of sketchy clubs where rich businessmen would take their barely-of-age girlfriends and sex workers to spend ludicrous sums on overpriced champagne. But this was something unexpected. Wandering the grounds, I found food trucks selling sandwiches and simple cocktails. Girls in long, flowery dresses swayed while guys with neck tattoos talked about their next big art projects on sex positivity. Never could I have imagined this kind of scene in old, conservative Ukraine.

After hours of non-stop dancing and loud conversations with strangers, I retreated to my hammock to recharge, listening to the quiet chatter around me. The sounds of the rave receded into the background and I began to drift off. Then, the DJ unleashed a series of bell-like tones, followed by a sudden drop to a deep bassline. My fatigue kept me from sensing the sudden change from soft, dreamy house to driving, hardcore techno. I closed my eyes and drowned in darkness, the beats from the 20 speakers flanking the stage pounding in my chest. Suddenly, my friends pulled me up. *Let's go!*

As I approached the scene, I saw hundreds of people in their 20s and 30s tearing up the improvised forest dancefloor. One raver was decked out in an intricate full-body suit made of ropes; others wore sports bras. All seemed united in a shared bliss, dancing to gritty techno music with broken beats and whispered voices. I waded through the crowd and reached the stage. I had never seen my fellow Ukrainians at complete liberty to do whatever, dance however they pleased and kiss whomever they wished. Even in Kyiv, a large metropolis of over 3 million people, such an open, relaxed atmosphere felt unimaginable. I threw my hands up to the sky alongside hundreds of fellow ravers and felt my feet sink deeper and deeper into the ground as I leapt into the air along with them. In response, the forest ground let loose a vast cloud of dust and sand. As it drifted back to the forest bed, it clung to our sweat-soaked skin and clothes. The warm air enfolded us, smelling of birch and dirt. We merged together. Soon, the sun would rise. But none of us wanted to go home.

...

In 1991, Ukraine emerged from the Cold War as a nation made very much in the authoritarian Soviet tradition. For decades, any sort of political activism meant a one-way ticket to the gulag. Suddenly, concepts like free speech and political dialogue were no longer verboten. But the fall of the Soviet Union also heralded an overnight conversion from communism to capitalism that wrought havoc on the country. An "every man for himself" mentality led to oligarchs like Rinat Akhmetov accruing vast, ill-gotten fortunes at the expense of the working-class and poor Ukrainians, who saw their meager savings evaporate. Simple survival consumed average Ukrainians, who had little time or capacity to contemplate how to exercise their new liberties. And the people remained wary about authority figures like the police: They have it out for us. Businessmen? They must be corrupt. Our politicians? They are all about nepotism and money. By the end of the 1990s, many Ukrainians, both young and old, viewed "politics" as dirty and corrupt. Trying to influence political change by voting or lobbying seemed futile, a feeling that persisted through the early 2000s as Ukrainians saw the political class fail, time and again, to rid the power structures of bribery and corruption. Then came Maidan.

On November 21, 2013, Viktor Yanukovych, then president of Ukraine, announced that he would not be signing a long-awaited pact to establish a political association and free trade with the European Union. Instead, he would opt for the Moscow-engineered Eurasian Economic Union, which would have ushered in economic integration with Russia. In protest, 1,500 students and activists flooded the streets, only to be attacked by the police. This triggered nationwide demonstrations and a massive, unprecedented, months-long rally on Kyiv's Independence Square, known as Maidan Nezalezhnosti, Over the course of the protests, more than 100 Ukrainians died at the hands of the berkut, a special police division that was later dismantled. In the end, Yanukovych fled for Russia, which would later annex Crimea illegally and begin its occupation of territory in the Donbas.

Following Maidan, younger Ukrainians came to feel their views on politics finally mattered. The Revolution of Dignity had unchained within the younger generation the realization

COMMUNIST KITSCH & HIPSTER CHIC

Some call Kyiv the **"NEW BERLIN."**

In 2021, its Zoloti Vorota district was voted one of Europe's coolest neighborhoods— above Amsterdam, Prague and Paris.

Ukrainian hipster nostalgia often has a nationalistic flavor.

TATTOOS OF MOLOTOV COCKTAILS, ANTI-TANK MISSILES & BREAD HELP SUPPORT THE WAR EFFORT.

Popular bands mix Ukrainian folk with rap and hip hop.

With patterned sofas and vintage knick-knacks, chain restaurant **SPOTYKACH** looks like a circa-1960s Soviet mother's home.

Embroidered peasant blouses are popular, along with kitschy track suits and granny glasses.

Heritage instruments like the trembita, an alpine horn up to 8 meters long, and bandura, a plucked string folk instrument with 68 strings, join electronic beats.

UNDERGROUND PARTIES ROCK ABANDONED FACTORIES.

Slogans like **"PUTIN IS A DICK"** or **"PRAY FOR UKRAINE"** adorn t-shirts.

---

that their views on politics and their voices counted. They had manned the frontlines of the revolution and represented the first generation born into an independent Ukraine, largely removed from the memories of Soviet oppression. "The children that had witnessed the Orange Revolution in 2004 were now, 10 years later, in their 20s, and they created their own vision of Ukrainian independence. They started to realize the power they possess," said Serhii Leshchenko, 42, former MP of the Ukrainian parliament, advisor to President Volodymyr Zelensky and long-time raver.

But the aftermath of Maidan also evoked anger and depression. The annexation of Crimea and the war in eastern Ukraine spurred an economic crisis, even as Ukraine took a more pro-European turn under President Petro Poroshenko. "It really influenced the emotional state of our people," Dmytro, 25, a DJ and producer who goes by the stage name of Badwor7h. "There will be more challenges ahead, so we have to bond together and create cultural institutions on the basis of our personal values," Vika, 26, a student at Mohylyanka University, who witnessed the revolution firsthand, told me.

That meant, in part, a cultural explosion, in the form of street art, electronic music and streetwear fashion. Unlike other scenes, where you either belonged or you didn't, the rave scene functioned as a meeting point for all these graffiti artists, designers and musicians, as well as activists, journalists and expats like me.

In late 2013, Serhii Yatsenko, Serhii Vel and Timur Basha, a trio of party promoters opened a club in an abandoned factory in Kyiv's Podil neighborhood, a one-time industrial hub. The club, named Closer, was a second home to the DJs and artists, both established and lesser-known, that they'd worked with over the years. At weekend-long parties, DJs at Closer played an eclectic blend of genres, including house, techno and hardbass. Its charm lay in its friendly "come as you are"

Nzyhoiurkivska Street, Kyiv. 2021. Photograph by Gueorgui Pinkhassov/Magnum.

atmosphere—a sentiment still foreign to a country that, for nearly 70 years, had suffocated under Soviet rule. Others soon followed in Closer's footsteps: Cxema, Club on Kyrylivskyj, Keller Bar, Arsenal XXII and organizations like Veselka and Rhythm Büro. "Closer inspired people," Vera, the cofounder of Rhythm Büro, told me. "We watched this cool project unfold and thought to ourselves—we can do this too!" By 2019, Podil had transformed into a vibrant artistic hub.

Like the forest rave, this was not an outwardly political environment. It was more a safe space where my peers could be themselves—even if, at times, that meant venting disappointment with a system some still felt was failing them. "There's a lot of anger in the music we play during these raves. The rooms are dark, and the installations look threatening. They reflect the reality, despite the fact that people go there to forget all about reality," Dmytro said.

...

During the summer of 2019, I was working grueling hours, which made me all the more prone to spending my nights meeting up with friends and partying to clear my head. Luckily for me, nights always seemed endless during the summertime in Kyiv, and it was never too late to make my way down to a party. Khreshchatyk—Kyiv's main boulevard—would be filled with music, bubbly chatter and throngs of people maneuvering their way between the street performers.

As I strolled past the tall, static buildings with their sand-colored stone façades and baroque-styled balconies, I reached the Independence Square. From there, I made my way down a slope surrounded by greenery that led to the Dnipro River. Careless youngsters were scattered alongside the riverbank, watching the sunset while they drank beer and enjoyed the occasional cool breeze that disrupted the summer heat. Then, they headed further north into Podil, Kyiv's party district.

Podil—or "Lower City"—sits on Kyiv's right bank, embraced by the Dnipro River on one side and a pocket of green, rolling hills on the other. Historically, this was the city of the working class and craftsmen. In the late nineteenth and early twentieth centuries, it gave birth to tile-, brick- and cement factories that were located on Kyrylivska Street. Later, during the Soviet era, it became home to a shipbuilding enterprise. In the 1990s, industry throughout Ukraine began to decline, and many of the factories were shut down and abandoned. For young people, the district's main attractions were the low housing prices and the run-down historical buildings that were remnants from its nineteenth century role as the city center.

One night, some friends and I wandered into HVLV, or Hvylovyj, a bar founded in 2015 by a group of pro-Ukrainian students from Mohylyanka University. They named it after Mykola Hvylovyj, the Ukrainian revolutionary poet known for his writing that argued for the inherent connection between politics and art. Following his death by suicide in 1933, the Soviet Union banned his work. At HVLV, people hang out during the day or pre-drink in the early evening before hitting the raves on Kyrylivska. It's a low-key, underground space. "Underground means non-commercial, not out for profit," said Vasyl, a 29-year-old event organizer at HVLV. "We're united in our common values and interests."

Every night, the dark basement, lit by a neon-purple haze of lights, filled up with ravers downing HVLV's infamous tequila shots. Layers of graffiti covered the bathroom doors (an example: "Why is Beyoncé singing 'to the left'? 'Cause women have no rights.") Tattoo artists, designers and musicians mingled with students, journalists and other free-thinking types, deep in shouted but cordial debates over art, LGBT rights and feminism. In a country where a woman's worth depended on her beauty, where people threw Molotov cocktails through the windows of gay bars, and where the most important thing in the world (as my ex-boss would say) was green dollar bills, it felt subversive and thrilling to hear. "The first rule of HVLV: Don't be a dickhead. That's the main threshold for people to even enter this place," Vasyl said with a grin. I laughed, but he was serious: a core tenet of the Podil scene is to create safe spaces—"a pretty new narrative in Ukraine," Ihor, a co-founder of Rhythm Büro, told me.

Clubs like HVLV, Closer and Keller often hire security guards to man their doors—in itself, not that unusual. But they'll often stop aggressive youngsters from going inside, as they might create problems for other party-goers, such as members of the LGBT community. In a country where it's customary to pay off a bouncer to gain entry into a club, this the idea of making basic decency the coin of the realm—"How open-minded do you seem and how likely are you to start harassing girls or beating up same-sex couples?"—was a radical concept. This safe space has allowed people to experiment with self-expression without fear of judgment or risk of oppression. It drew in more and more

COME FOR THE MUSIC, STAY FOR THE POLITICS

"The Eurovision Song Contest shall in no case be politicised." —Eurovision's official rules

Since 2013, Russia has consistently been booed over its anti-gay laws and incursions into Ukraine.

GEORGIA'S 2009 ENTRY, "WE DON'T WANNA PUT IN," WAS RULED A POLITICAL DIG AT PUTIN. RATHER THAN CHANGE IT, THEY WITHDREW.

In 2017, host city Kyiv temporarily turned its Friendship of Nations Arch into a rainbow to honor the theme "Celebrate Diversity," sparking anti-gay protests.

UKRAINE WON IN 2016, 2 YEARS AFTER RUSSIA'S ANNEXATION OF CRIMEA. THE SONG, "1944," DESCRIBED THE DEPORTATION OF THE CRIMEAN TATARS BY JOSEPH STALIN.

Russia's 2017 contestant was banned from Ukraine (where the contest was held) for performing in occupied Crimea. Russia withdrew and Ukraine was threatened with sanctions.

IN 2019, ICELAND WAS FINED FOR HOLDING UP SCARVES IN SUPPORT OF PALESTINE.

In 2021, after Brexit was finalized, the United Kingdom received **ZERO POINTS**.

In 2022, Russia was banned after invading Ukraine. Ukraine won.

people from Ukraine's middle class, and organizers rapidly saw their public double or triple.

That's what makes the underground scene in Kyiv so unique: none of the people who frequent it have a simplistic "fuck the system" in mind. Instead, they are more nuanced. They believe in a brighter future for Ukraine. And they seem to be building a foundation for it within the confines of this underground safe space, where they can be who and whatever they want to be. The Podil scene is instrumental in uniting these people, allowing them to express themselves and subsequently spread the liberal values they encounter here through all of Kyiv, a city that is now learning to thrive in this new sense of openness and creativity. It has coaxed Kyiv out of the memories of dictatorship and oligarchy into something more modern and open-minded.

• • •

What, then, are the politics of Podil?

Many members of the underground rave scene dismiss the very idea that the scene emerged as a response to the political turbulence that took place in 2014. The founders and organizers of Closer, Rhythm Büro and HVLV claim that the timing of their formation was purely coincidental. "Right after Maidan, there was chaos," Ihor said. "And in this environment, it was more comfortable to develop nightlife than it was under an iron fist. But I wouldn't say that there's a direct causal link between Maidan and nightlife."

HVLV also remains adamant about its apolitical stance. Being political, in their view, would imply supporting a political party or an oligarch, espousing opinions on gas prices or pushing for reforms in spheres like education, economic policy or the legal system. At HVLV, I noticed slogans on their courtyard walls: "Police should protect, not torture" and "Avakov has to go," a reference to Ukraine's previous corrupt minister of affairs. One of the beers they have on tap is called ACAB, for "All Craftlovers Ale Beautiful," but that also mirrors an acronym for the English political slogan "All Cops Are Bastards." "That's not political activism, though," Vasyl said. "It's social activism."

The assertion puzzled me. How could anyone in these spaces see themselves as apolitical? Yet given the history of this place, it makes sense. Generations of Ukrainians living under Communism only knew a one-party system, where personal and political thoughts could only be voiced, literally, underground: in the basements or private kitchens of their homes, in hushed tones. As a result, in modern Ukraine, "being political" is often conflated with the idea of "politically involved." As Vasyl explained, concepts like human rights, tolerance, mutual respect and being pro-choice and LGBT-friendly occupy a separate realm from politics. They're seen as distinct social issues.

But others dismiss the notion that the underground scene can be seen as detached from politics. "These people are lying to themselves. They are the products of political changes," Serhii Leshchenko said. "Democracy and raves are synonyms. Raves embody the right to self-expression. There are no raves in non-democratic countries. Self expression isn't possible in authoritarian communities."

As the war with Russia rages on, I'm left to wonder how long this scene can maintain its apolitical stance. In Kyiv's rave scene, most DJs and producers, finally working again since Russian forces retreated from the capitol, refused to play Russian music in their sets. According to Leshchenko, Russian EDM is canceled. "The future looks more anti-Russian. DJs won't be using Russian producers anymore, but rather choose to mix Ukrainian patriotic songs into their sets." "For many years, I tried to stick to the idea that I was apolitical," Dmytro told me. "Until the start of the war, that idea remained untouched. But now I realize it's infantile; you have to pick a side."

• • •

August 27, 2022. More than six months after Russia's full-scale invasion into Ukraine, Dmytro and I walk down Kyrylivska Street through the sweltering summer heat. Curfew in Kyiv starts at 11 p.m., so these raves can't last through the night anymore. But in typical Ukrainian "to hell with it" fashion, clubs open their doors during the daytime.

The factory buildings appear to be crumbling. We take a sharp left and walk up a path surrounded by trees and bushes, in stark contrast to the industrialized feel of the street. A worn metal gate opens as we come closer. "No pictures or videos," the ticket girl says as she covers my phone camera with a silver heart-shaped sticker.

Hidden in the depths of Podil, Keller Club was hailed as the underground place of the moment right before Russia attacked on February 24. I walk down the wooden stairs and make my way to a courtyard that has been turned into a makeshift dance floor. In the center stands a DJ, a big, steel cube adorned with ivy plants hanging over him. A loud, angry bassline thunders out of the speakers, demanding that we dance. No one can resist the aggressive beats blasting through the stereo. This isn't just dancing; it's jumping, sweating, screaming as if our lives depend on it.

"You'd think the DJs are sparing them, but they need it even harder," Dmytro says as he gazes into the mad stampede that is unfolding in front of us. I sip my drink and nod quietly. Never have I seen such peace in the wake of such aggression. It's like seeing a poison being drained from a wound. It's exactly what Ukraine needs. ❋

STRANGER'S GUIDE

NATIONAL MAGAZINE AWARD WINNER

FOR GENERAL EXCELLENCE & PHOTOGRAPHY

MY DRAG NAME IS MORE, but my family name is Moe—so More comes from Moe.

I majored in ballet, but in Korea, men have to go into the military, and when I quit university, I really didn't want to go into the army. I am transgender, and it took more than a year to prove I was transgender to the army.

I identify as pangender. I'm not gay. I always wanted to be a beautiful woman. But after I met my husband, and he loved me so much, I decided not to change; not to have surgery. But today, when people ask me, I just say, "I am a human, I just want to be a beautiful human."

"Mo" in Chinese characters is "hair." But it sounds like my name. "Re" in Chinese characters is "fish." So MoRe is "hairy fish" in Chinese characters. That's how I think of myself in society: kind of like a hairy fish.

MORE *Drag queen & dancer, South Korea*

STRANGER'S GUIDE BRINGS YOU FACE TO FACE WITH PEOPLE AROUND THE WORLD

With every volume of *Stranger's Guide*, you'll meet new people like More, who share their hopes and realities, all in their own words. Go beyond the stories and gain a deeper understanding of locations around the world through local perspectives. With *Stranger's Guide*, you can stay globally engaged and experience new places, all without leaving your home.

STRANGERSGUIDE.COM/SUBSCRIBE

A Brief History of Ukrainian Independence

FEBRUARY 2010

Viktor Yanukovych, Putin's favored candidate, is elected president after saying the country should be a "neutral state" cooperating with Russia and the West.

FEBRUARY 2014

Violence continues into the new year. Yanukovych flees to Russia and is charged with mass murder. Parliament votes to remove him from office. Yanukovych, and later Russia, declare it an illegal coup.

MARCH–SEPTEMBER 2014

Russia occupies the Crimean Peninsula, and the Crimean parliament votes to secede from Ukraine and join Russia. The U.S. and its European allies impose sanctions on Russia. Violence breaks out in the Donbas region, and Russian separatists take Donetsk and Luhansk, declaring independence from Ukraine. Western ally Petro Poroshenko becomes president of Ukraine. A ceasefire with Russia is signed—and broken.

2016

By the end of the year, more than 1,200 Lenin monuments have been taken down, and almost 1,000 towns and villages have had their names changed from those associated with communism.

2016

Public servants are made to declare their assets (including income, real estate, bank accounts...and the number of fur coats they own) via an electronic database each year.

2017

Ukraine bans the "unauthorized distribution" of Russian books.

APRIL 2013

In response to censorship and media monopolization, journalist and democracy activist Mustafa Nayyem launches Hromadske.tv, Ukraine's first independent Internet TV channel, funded by donations.

NOVEMBER 2013

Days before signing an EU association agreement, Yanukovych backs out, leading to the Euromaidan Protests, the largest protests in Ukraine since the Orange Revolution of 2004–2005. Demonstrators in Kyiv's Maidan Square chant: "Ukraine is Europe."

2014

A wave of Ukrainian literature is published—much of it political—in a backlash against Russian publishers. There is a rise in Ukrainian "patriotic cinema," supported and subsidized by the state.

2014–2015

The post-Maidan government leads a fight against the dominance of Russian popular culture in Ukraine. These culture wars are known as *Kulturkampf*, borrowed from the German movement of the 1800s.

APRIL 2015

Ukraine's parliament passes "decommunization" legislation, banning promotion of its communist past. This includes the hammer and sickle flag used by the Ukrainian Soviet Socialist Republic from 1950 to 1992.

2015

The National Anti-Corruption Bureau of Ukraine launches. Among its targets: the incumbent head of tax administration. It's a big step considering that, for so long following the collapse of the Soviet Union, oligarchical control of institutions have been a roadblock to progress.

APRIL 2019

Comedian Volodymyr Zelensky is elected president in a landslide.

SEPTEMBER 2019

After years of enduring attempts at blocking any real judicial reform, in September, President Zelensky announces a meeting to prevent his plans to clean up the judicial system from being sabotaged.

2021

President Zelensky bans three TV channels from the list of those allowed to be distributed in the country.

2022

Volunteers scramble to preserve Ukrainian websites, videos, posters, images and music before the servers and computers that host them are destroyed in the ongoing war.

Conflicts of Interest

Building a democratic media in Ukraine

Laura Secor

When Anastacia Stanko was born, the Soviet empire had only four years left to live. It would not be much missed in her native city of Ivano-Frankivsk. There, certain Ukrainian traditions had never stopped breathing where they lay buried. There was a banned scouts group and the long-suppressed Greek Catholic church. Pictures of Stanko in young adulthood showed her in national costume, against the Ukrainian nationalist colors red and black. Her family owned a small business that built hearths. There was a river where she liked to swim, and a sister just a year behind her, and a conservative school that drew from a wellspring of anti-Soviet, Ukrainian patriotism.

In 2004, when Stanko was a journalism student in Lviv, she took part in the Orange Revolution, protesting the installation of a pro-Russian ex-con named Viktor Yanukovich as president. She believed that behind her orange banner was the cause her grandmother had fought for as a nationalist partisan in the Second World War. The Orange Revolution succeeded, but its political leaders were weak. Power gravitated where it always had: toward money, which was concentrated in the hands of oligarchs, and toward Russia, which riddled Ukraine's ship of state with holes. Yanukovich, who had made his first living stealing women's hats, ran a divisive campaign in 2010 and won. His popular support came mainly from the country's predominantly Russian-speaking east.

New protests, bigger and angrier, erupted ten years after the orange ones. Their epicenter was Maidan Nezalezhnosti, Kyiv's vast central square. Now Stanko was a media pioneer, a co-founder of the country's first independent television newsroom, known as Hromadske. She live-streamed the protests by day, edited at night, slept for maybe three hours at a stretch. She channeled the square's wild energy, she stoked it, she became famous. People called her station the voice of Maidan. There were peaceful encampments, and there were riot police, and

A volunteer retrieves documents that Yanukovich dumped into the lake when he fled Ukraine. Mezhyhirya, near Kyiv. 2014. Photograph by Mikhail Pochuyev/SIPA.

eventually there were street clashes, Molotov cocktails, burning buildings, gunshots, national shock and grief. Yanukovich fled. Stanko thought she would finally sleep.

Instead she went to war. Russia annexed Crimea and then made a play for a swath of eastern Ukraine. In the spring and summer of 2014, Stanko's friends from her childhood scouts group joined volunteer battalions fighting Russians and separatists in the country's industrial eastern region known as Donbas. She followed them with a camera. Her first reports had an eccentric quality. With her flak jacket and helmet she wore pink pants, a tank top, sandals. She shouted sometimes, mugged for the camera, and grinned like she could barely hold back some vaguely transgressive joke. She wasn't a combat reporter, but she became one.

On June 30, 2014, Stanko and her cameraman were taken prisoner by separatists behind the frontline in Luhansk. In captivity she had little choice but to listen to people very different from herself, who saw the country's agony in a completely opposing light. She tried to understand what they saw. This act of imagination lit a spark of change in her. She began to think that the country needed open dialogue as much as it needed anything else. So much was never talked about, even from the bloody twentieth century, and so there was no shared understanding of history, only winners and losers. By January 2015, Stanko, when on camera, no longer appeared to be out on a lark with a group of heavily armed friends. Instead, she entered bomb shelters or crowds of angry civilians whose shattered homes were five degrees Celsius indoors, and who demanded food, water and security. She was the reporter following Ukrainian troops in retreat and repeatedly asking how many were dead. She went to mental hospitals and prisons in the conflict zone, documenting lives trapped or forgotten. Though she covered Russian abuses and manipulations in the conflict region, Stanko also covered those from her own side: ceasefire violations, prisoners held incommunicado, collateral damage. She presented the suffering of civilians and soldiers with an unflinching humanity devoid of romance or jingoism. She believed she was doing her job, which was to hold up a mirror to her inflamed country, in the hope that it could see itself whole.

...

Russia shocked much of the world by invading Ukraine in February 2022, but Ukrainians already understood themselves to be at war with Russia since 2014, and, in fact, the fighting had been continuous. From 2014 to 2022, dozens of soldiers and civilians died every month in Donbas, where forces dug into trenches battled across a volatile line of contact and civilians sought ever-elusive reprieve. Two agreements negotiated in Minsk were meant to pacify the conflict but did nothing of the kind, as Russia-backed separatists continually violated their terms. The existence on Ukrainian territory of regions outside the government's control, with citizens Kyiv could neither support nor protect, was destabilizing by design.

It was during this period, in 2017, that I visited Kyiv and Kharkiv. Both were vibrant, meticulously tended cities: Kyiv, of pastel facades and gilded cupolas on steep and winding streets whose every berm was planted in flowers; Kharkiv, of cosmopolitan universities, vast squares and monuments to Soviet-era constructivism. The people I met in both cities were absorbed in the business of self-government after Maidan. The Ukraine they occupied felt at once far from the front and tethered to it, as Ukrainian civil society struggled to balance its embrace of democratic pluralism against the designs of an enemy determined to exploit any fissure.

When I met Stanko in 2017, many of the people who had loved her reporting from Maidan seemed to hate her reports from Donbas. On social media, some said she had Stockholm Syndrome. They said she was soft on Russia. They called her names. "Journalist-whore Stanko needs to be prosecuted and jailed for separatism," read a typical Facebook post at the time. She got text messages identifying her address and telling her to be careful, because anything could happen. That she used the phrase "the Ukrainian army" instead of "our army" proved her a traitor, said some: A journalist—maybe—could aspire to be even-handed, though her critics doubted even this. But a patriot could not. She was exhausted by it.

As the chief editor of Hromadske East, her station's program on the conflict zone, during those years Stanko sat at the intersection of her country's two defining struggles. One was the war in Donbas where, even then, Ukraine fought a lopsided contest with Russia not only over territory but for the proverbial hearts and minds of a whipsawed population. The other was the effort of young people like Stanko to make good on the promise of the 2014 Maidan revolution: liberal reform and government transparency, both of which require a robust and critical free press.

Reform alone would have been a hefty agenda for a country with a chronic, deep-rooted corruption problem. But the war, even before last winter's full-scale invasion, made things more complicated still. Portrayed by a relentless Russian media machine as an apocryphal nation under fascist control, Ukraine expended enormous energy simply in defining itself and trying to show its best face to a skeptical world. Some Ukrainian patriots saw a media that insisted on exposing the country's warts and criticizing its government as counterproductive in that effort. Others believed that such a press was exactly what the country was fighting for.

Frontline near Occupied Bal-akliya Kharkiv region. 2022. Photograph by Marcin Suden.

Before Maidan, Ukraine had long had a lively and fractious media, without its ever being exactly free. Oligarchs owned the television networks, television was king and the whims, vanities and feuds of the station owners dictated newsroom priorities and marked off taboos. Back in 2012, Yanukovich had briefly replaced even this imperfect quorum with a heavy-handed unanimity in the Russian style. The 2014 Maidan revolution released that grip, but as with so much else in Ukraine, corruption remained the media's besetting sin. Politicians paid for favorable content, and oligarchs kept reporters well fed while using newsrooms as instruments of personal influence.

The name "Hromadske" meant "public": it was adopted by about a dozen disgruntled reporters from the oligarchic networks in 2013, when they set about establishing a nonprofit television station that was meant to serve the public interest and to prize professional standards above all. Stanko got in on the ground floor, having met Hromadske's other co-founders in an anti-censorship campaign that linked independent-minded journalists during Yanukovich's time.

With limited resources from foreign funders, Stanko and her colleagues expected to start airing weekly episodes online in November 2013. But the station's launch date coincided with the start of demonstrations on Maidan, and Hromadske instead began live-streaming 24 hours a day, seven days a week, often from reporters' iPhones, while also hosting discussions in its makeshift studio. The production values were poor, but the subject was urgent and the material uncensored. Ukrainians all over the world tuned in—at a given moment on November 24, 2013, the new station logged more than 760,000 simultaneous viewers—and Stanko, with her characteristic squint and rabbit-toothed smile, was one of its most recognizable correspondents.

For Stanko and her colleagues, Hromadske and Maidan were the stuff of dreams. They worked without looking over their shoulders for the first time in their professional lives, and they did it, seemingly, with everybody watching. The new station streamed on YouTube and trended on Twitter because these were the platforms available. But the content was old school, and the staff was made up of trained professionals in a country whose press corps skewed young.

Stanko later looked back on the four months of Maidan as though they were a continuous day, spent moving from street to studio to street again. Events unspooled at a furious pace. In central Kyiv, tires burned into dense black smoke while activists faced off with rows of helmeted, shielded riot police. When security forces threw activists from the top of a colonnade at the entrance to a sports stadium, Stanko was there, streaming. Two days after the worst violence against the protesters, President

Grey Zone between the frontlines, near Kharkiv. 2022. Photograph by one of the colonels.

Yanukovich fled the country, and journalists invaded Mezhyhiria, his lavish, 350-acre estate outside of Kyiv, at whose gates reporters used to mass yearly in a ritual demand for entry. Now for the first time it lay exposed: the gilded house, the private zoo, the ostrich farm, the spa, the bowling alley, the restaurant, the salt cave, the food laboratory. As he fled, Yanukovich and his aides dumped hundreds of documents into the lake that edged the property. Volunteer divers retrieved them, teams of journalists laid them out on the helicopter pad to dry and restore. Stanko imagined she would have fodder to investigate Yanukovich's abuses for years to come.

But within the week, Russian gunmen appeared in Crimea, where pro-Russian rebels seized control of the capital. Stanko was in the Hromadske studio the night it became evident that Russia was taking the peninsula away. A colleague hid her backpack to keep her from rushing to the scene. She would be conspicuous in Crimea. She spoke Ukrainian as her primary language, was not comfortable speaking Russian, and worked for a media organization strongly associated with the revolution that was Moscow's pretext for rescuing Russian-speaking citizens from the fascist junta that it alleged had just seized power in Kyiv.

To be on the safe side, on reaching the first administrative checkpoint on the Crimean peninsula, Stanko tore her Hromadske press card into pieces and ate it. But no harm came to her in Crimea. She thought the atmosphere was surreal, and that local people believed in fairy tales invented by the Russian media—like that Right Sector, a far right Ukrainian nationalist group that was active on Maidan, had stationed anti-aircraft mounts and chemical weapons in the Crimean mountains, or that if they voted in a referendum to join Russia, the Kremlin would give them all free apartments like in Soviet times. Then she crossed back to the mainland, and saw Ukrainian soldiers digging trenches, and understood that whatever else was artifice, her country was at war.

...

Ukraine was an early laboratory for Russian manipulation of a sort that became familiar to Americans only later. Among the narratives Moscow had promoted to help Yanukovich come to power in the first place was one of stark division between residents of eastern and western Ukraine. Russian propaganda would have you believe that Western Ukrainians were crypto-fascists who looked down on the Russian-speaking Crimeans and Eastern Ukrainians. By its lights, Eastern Ukrainians, especially in industrial Donbas, were unrefined, inferior—or, if you were an Eastern Ukrainian, the hard-working salt of the earth. Russia pushed the line that Maidan, when it came, was a CIA-sponsored coup d'etat that installed a Nazi government in Kyiv. Yet it was also a decadent street party held by people who didn't like to work. Moscow's spinmasters accused Ukraine of being a failed (but fascist) state with an abusive army pummeling the Russian-speakers whom Westerners despised. That Kyiv was itself a largely Russian-speaking city seemed merely an inconvenience to the purveyors of these tangled stories, as confusion, not coherence, was the object.

Before 2014, Russian television had near total penetration of the Ukrainian market. No language barrier existed, and even Ukrainian channels borrowed footage from their Russian counterparts. The media market was porous. After 2014, it could not afford to be: Russia was an enemy at war for Ukraine's autonomy and its territory, using its much larger, richer, top-down media to pummel its neighbor with information offensives designed to tear its society apart and cause its democratic government to fail. In the first years after Maidan, the Ukrainian government under then-President Petro Poroshenko took action, blocking Russian television signals and banning Russian social media companies from Ukrainian space. At the time of my visit, these measures were controversial. Were they the minimum required for the country's self-defense? Or were they akin to censorship?

Viktoria Syumar, a member of parliament with a background in journalism, made the case for the measures to me in stark terms. The Russian media, as she described it then, was not competing in any marketplace of ideas. Rather, it was a coordinated instrument of coercion indistinguishable from the Kremlin. To simply leave the Ukrainian populace to sort real journalism from malevolent libels would not suffice. "We have some people who lived in the Soviet Union," she said. "They believe that everything they can watch on TV is true. We don't have in our educational system criticism, we don't have media literacy, we don't have any political education." Fixing this was certainly a priority. But in the meantime, Russia could not be permitted to manipulate Ukrainians at will.

As a democracy, Ukraine did not have a top-down propaganda machine, and the media it did have, in its diversity and absence of state control, could not be weaponized. But hybrid war presented journalists with unavoidable moral questions. Were Ukrainian reporters obligated to consider the possible misuses of the information they produced? Was it their job to promote an opposing narrative to the Russian one? Did it even make a difference? "I guess if you have an opponent with a huge machine worth $4 billion per year and directed by a whole system of state authorities, media experts [in Ukraine] will not be able to do anything," Syumar said. "It's like an insect punching an elephant."

Such was the dilemma that faced Ukrainian war correspondents like Stanko during what turned out to be the conflict's low ebb. The model for public television in Ukraine was originally the BBC: journalism that was not in the pocket of an oligarch or a president, that was not for sale or for use or for Russia, would adopt the standards of the British broadcaster, reporting both sides, evincing neutrality, staring down unpleasant truths, showing no favor. But what sounded high-minded in principle in 2013 rubbed even some liberal-minded Ukrainians wrong when they felt their country under existential threat. By 2017, "BBC standards" had become a term not of aspiration but of abuse. "BBC standards," spoken with implicit scare quotes, was reporting on your own war as though it were happening to someone else, it was prizing balance over country and neutrality over one's own side. "BBC standards," as a former colleague of Stanko's put it to me, meant taking a vegetarian position in the face of aggression in war.

A country that on Maidan seemed very certain it wanted a free press sometimes appeared to have buyers' remorse in the years that immediately followed. Tatyana Lebedeva, the head of a commission that successfully transformed Ukraine's formerly state-owned broadcaster into a large public one, told me in 2017 that Ukrainian journalists were too negative: they should temper their investigative work with more positive stories about the government. "These might be success stories, stories of some heroes, something motivational," Lebedeva said. "This sort of information is crucial for people, especially in times of war, as without it they can fall into depression."

Nataliya Ligachova, who ran Ukraine's media watchdog, an NGO called Detektor Media, agreed: "There should be a very delicate balance between criticizing and presenting positive information about the transformation going on inside the country, sometimes supporting the authorities, especially in foreign policy and concerning the response to external aggression." According to Ligachova, Ukrainian journalists had to weigh their professional duties against their civic ones. Stanko's station, Hromadske, she said, "sometimes even cross the line on that, in the sense that sometimes under the guise of impartiality they introduce criticism."

The notion of patriotism as precluding criticism, and of the press as responsible for bucking up the national mood and refraining from undermining the authorities, seemed less prevalent among the younger Ukrainian media professionals, who were reared in post-Soviet times. Ukraine had one of the region's most vibrant investigative press corps, and particularly after Maidan, journalists saw ferreting out official corruption as a patriotic duty to their country's better future. That future would be starkly differentiated from Russia's, not least in Ukraine's embrace of a spirit of critical pluralism. To this extent, a noisy, fractious, even oppositional press corps would be no mosquito, but something far more potent in confronting the Russian elephant.

"What was completely unacceptable for Mr. Putin and his crowd was Ukraine's success on a different road to the future," Evgeny Kisilev, a well-known Russian opposition journalist living in Kyiv, told me. "Ukraine's success as a country which develops along the lines of a multi-political, multicultural, pro-Western model and road of development would be a very significant blow to Vladimir Putin's political practices. And it could have been a vivid example to the Russian population and Russian citizens, that you don't necessarily need to wage a new cold war against the West to be a successful nation. You don't necessarily need to limit democratic rights and freedoms to be a successful nation."

Many liberal Ukrainians of Stanko's generation argued that Ukraine could defeat Russia's propaganda campaign not by manipulating the flow of information, but by making a better truth prevail. If the standard of living in Ukraine was higher than that in Russia, if the press was freer, if civil liberties were respected, if the tireless efforts of civil society succeeded in checking the government's staggering levels of graft, then no one would need convincing that Maidan was, as its supporters called it, a "Revolution of Dignity," and that the Russian media peddled malicious lies.

In February 2022, Russia took to shelling Ukraine's lovingly tended cities and massacring civilians in a campaign it all but announced as genocide. In doing so, it ceded the information war to Ukraine, but in a manner that would afford the country's courageous press corps little comfort. One of the investigative reporters I'd met in Kyiv led a tank unit into battle in Donbas. Others posted from bomb shelters and from cities aflame. Stanko considered joining the Territorial Defense, but in the end continued doing what she had always done: She accompanied soldiers into battle, captured unguarded moments of courage and grief, documented the lives of civilians under siege and exhumed the villages that Russia laid waste. Under the pitiless light of Russian artillery, the earlier debates about the role of the media in Ukraine might seem an irrelevance or a luxury. And yet for me, they still resonate as the expression of something essential about Ukraine's struggle and what it is fighting to defend. ✻

Scenes From the War

The diary of a Ukrainian Journalist

Anastasia Stanko

TRANSLATED BY
Olena Jennings

A month ago, my best friend died. In truth, I went to the front because he was there. A friend in the military called to tell me the news, but I didn't pick up the phone in time. When I looked at my phone, I saw that there were two missed calls. When you have two missed calls from a man on the front, it is clear right away—your friend is dead.

A month ago, there were a lot of dead. Every day another person I knew. Every day. I returned a missed call. Every day I was told what I already knew: that Vitalik was dead. I was shaken, but I did not cry. I had a tactical medicine training class to get to, and I didn't want to be late. That same evening, I had tickets to a stand-up comedy show where my husband was supposed to meet me.

I was making a tourniquet in class while I tried to solve my dilemma: would it be okay to go to stand-up comedy when Vitalik was dead? Would it be okay to laugh when they were transporting Vitalik to the morgue in Bakhmut? Would I find anything funny when my friend was going to identify the body? Was I spending my time wisely when it turns out the morgue in Bakhmut didn't have space for Vitalik's body, and only later, I would find out he had to lie for three days outside in the sun, because there were too many bodies to keep in the morgue. They had to bury him in a closed casket.

Before the show, my husband and I ate well at a buffet, and then at the show, we laughed. Do you understand how absurd this is? I wanted to disappear, to fall away, stop living, stop breathing, even more to simply stop eating, stop laughing. But what choice do you have? You are alive.

...

My mom came to visit me in Kyiv. My mom likes sushi, so we went to a spot for sushi. While we were eating, my brother called to tell us they were sending him to the Eastern front. My dad was already fighting. My mom was now all tears and sniffles. So was I. What are we supposed to do? Eat sushi? Then my mom stops crying and turns to me.

"You know what we should do?' she said.

"What?" I say.

"We should ride the Ferris wheel," she smiles. "But first, let's go buy some wine." So we went on this Ferris wheel, drank wine and reminisced about everything—and some things in particular. We even laughed.

...

Intimacy with my husband is difficult these days. I am always thinking of the stories of Ukrainian women and children being raped by Russian soldiers. I can't stop myself. My husband and I had to let go of our dreams. Before the war we had wanted to buy a bigger apartment, for us to live with our small son. We even went so far as to invest in a really nice neighborhood, with playgrounds, a pool and trees and greenery everywhere. But at the end of March, our future neighborhood was shelled. Our future apartment didn't suffer, but we decided to give it up anyway; we'll never get back part of the money. But we always joke that we survived those first six months of war very pleasantly.

My husband is a reserve officer. Every day, we talk about how lucky we are that we are alive and well. But we also talk about what will happen if he is drafted. We can't help but tell the darkest jokes; they all circle around death. We laugh. Then we talk about what will happen if I die. Here, the joke is always the same. If I die, my husband won't be mobilized, because he will be the single father of a small child. Problem solved. We laugh again. We are especially glad that our son doesn't understand anything. He is, thankfully, too young. But he is growing, and the war continues. We don't think about the future anymore.

...

I travel again to report from the front.

The worst moment is when I have to hug Ostap goodbye. He clings to me with his tiny hands. And doesn't want to let go. I don't cry, ever. But every time at this moment, I think: if I die, my child will be left without a mother. This is irresponsible.

In July 2021, I decided to quit my job as a journalist and dedicate my time to my six-month-old son. Then on July 23, 2022, I went to the independent media channel, Hromadske, and offered my services as a war correspondent, in case something started. I thought that not doing this was irresponsible.

I now spend close to two weeks a month on the front and two weeks at home. Every time I take a trip, it is about 1000 kilometers there and back. Every time, I both want and don't want to go to the front, and every time, I think I might die. At the same time I think that it's irresponsible to leave my small child a half orphan.

Every time, when I wait for a long time near the front for permission and papers to do my work, I think: God, what am I doing here? Who needs this reporting? It would be better if I studied tactical medicine, maybe then I would save someone.

...

The truth is I am frightened.

It is more frightening than the beginning of 2014 in Donbas, more frightening than when I was held prisoner in separatist captivity, more frightening than in 2016 in Avdiika, when two soldiers died in front of me.

I ran away from a position on the front a few days ago; the very position I had asked to be allowed to go to with my videographer. My throat was already dry when we arrived at the spot to report. I got out of the car and was informed that I still needed to walk another kilometer and a half to the final position. I had a panic attack and just left the videographer there. A month earlier, I had been close to this same spot, walking just the last kilometer to my position when we were shelled. There was no other choice but to turn and walk back to the car through the shelling. That was the most frightening hour of my life. As I walked, I took hold of the hand of the general who was leading us. I had convinced myself that a rocket would hardly dare kill the general. He had experience, and if I was with him, I'd be okay. You tell yourself lies so as not to drive yourself crazy with fear.

...

What saves you most from fear is shame.

Shame when you face people—military or civilians, doctors, police or firefighters—people who continue to do their work no matter what. They hold onto their weapons and shovels and stay at their positions. When they are fired at from all sides, they fly forward into smoke and explosions, they evacuate the wounded, perform surgery while rushing to the hospital. They pull a neighbor out of the rubble of a building when it is about to collapse, they share food and water, they feed the cats and dogs of an entire high-rise building when all the residents have left, and they don't leave, because "To whom will I leave all of this?"

It's shameful to be weak. It's shameful to be frightened.

Every Ukrainian feels shame. There's no need to instruct us from New York, Quebec or Berlin about what is the right way to act during war.

Those who left are ashamed because everyone else stayed. Those who didn't leave are ashamed because they moved or live in relatively quieter regions, where there is less shelling. Those who live in dangerous regions are ashamed that they aren't volunteering. Those who are volunteering are ashamed that they aren't fighting. Those who took up arms are ashamed that it isn't in the most threatened city. And so it goes, on and on. Beyond the shame, there is hate. Hate toward Russia and its citizens. Hate of the Belarusians.

...

There are still some thorny discussions about "good Russians." There is a joke these days that the only good Russian is a dead Russian. Some people debate whether we ought to hold some kind of dialogue with those Russians who are against the war—because Russia will always be a neighbor: our large neighbor with its population of 145 million. How do you establish a dialogue with someone who gets a tattoo that says "no war" and thinks that they did enough? It is incomprehensible. And they think that they are risking a lot getting such a tattoo. Some of them don't even write "no war," but instead wrote "** ***." Meanwhile, Ukrainians risk our lives simply by living in our homes.

What does this "no war" mean? That everyone must simply stop firing and go home? Will the Russians who simply stop firing go? Will they leave all our lands, or only what was taken after February 24, 2022? And what about our people, kidnapped and taken thousands of miles away, far into Russia? How are they faring? What about our dead, the ones buried in the yards of their own houses? What about our violated men and women? What about our stolen grain? The stolen tractors? The looted paintings in museums?

...

All of those who claim to be wise and moral, those who always claimed to be for rights, democracy and freedom are starting to make me angry. Especially the Western liberal media.

The New York Times decided to open a bureau in Kyiv. A wonderful idea. Finally, they are trying to find out what is happening in Ukraine from Ukraine. Earlier everyone tried to find out about Ukraine from the Moscow bureau. Seriously. In 2002, there was the Sknyliv air show disaster near Lviv. At an air show, a plane crashed onto the spectators. 77 people were killed; more than 250 were wounded. Where did the Western media write about this? From the bureau in Moscow. But enough of this. The same thing is true of *The Washington Post*. Isabelle Khurshudyan, who will be heading the office here, also worked in the Moscow bureau.

"Is it necessary for you to have experience in London to write articles from Mumbai, or experience working in Paris to write about Algiers?" my colleague on the appointment of a Moscow journalist to work in the Kyiv bureau. This is an example of a usual assumption that Ukraine is somewhere in Russia's shadow, in its orbit, in its sphere of influence, and that if you lived and worked in Moscow and know Russia, then you will easily assimilate here in Kyiv.

...

I am often glad that my grandmother and grandfather didn't live to see this war. My father's parents each spent 10 years in the Gulag. They met and married in Magadan, where they were exiled after Stalin's death. They hated Russia all of their long lives, even though my grandfather had to fight in the Soviet Army, liberating Europe from fascism.

My grandmother was 10 years old when her father was killed in the war, near Berlin. He also fought in the Soviet Army. The death notice came on May 9, 1945, exactly on Victory Day. We never celebrated this day in our family. After Victory Day, my great grandmother lived with three kids in a bombed-out house where she did her best to run the household. But the Soviet powers took everything she had: the horse, the cow, the pig, even their passports. They were the newest serfs.

...

I remember a story from my childhood that my mother would tell. When she was little, she went to a Soviet school. One day at home, she was telling her father about the history lessons they had learned in school. It was all about the 1930s and Soviet collectivization, the New Economic Policy that led to plentiful harvests and grand industrialization. My grandfather shook his head and told her that no, those years in Ukraine was the time of the Holodomor, when people were starving so badly that they ate their own children. Mother raised her eyebrows, not believing her own father, because there was nothing like that in the history books. It wasn't until the Soviet Union

Vitaly. Near Popasna in the Luhansk region. 2022. Photograph by Vitaly.

fell that she understood that her father was right, and the history books lied. And our whole lives were a lie.

I think about this now, traveling to report from the Kharkiv oblast.

• • •

Kharkiv was the second largest city in Ukraine before the war, with 1.4 million residents located about 35 kilometers from the Russian border. During nearly six months of active military action, there were only 10 days in which Kharkiv wasn't shelled.

In the city, it's impossible to ignore the war. It has touched every part of the city and left destroyed buildings everywhere. In March 2022, there were hardly any people in the streets. All those who didn't leave lived in basements or in the subway. They ventured out only to go home and wash up, or get something to feed their pets, or to run to the store or to get humanitarian aid.

Finally in May, life in the city returned a bit. I even found myself at a concert one day. The Ukrainian military freed 23 villages around Kharkiv, and the residents who had left started to think about returning. But a week later, the Russians didn't gain their position; they began shelling again, but this time with more intensity. Now there isn't a day when someone in Kharkiv doesn't die from shelling.

I head to the front, just two villages from Kharkiv. Just as I arrive, a tank is firing, a mine-thrower is firing and there are air strikes all at the same time. On the road to the hotel, I see an open shop that isn't a grocery store. Kharkiv is now a city of broken windows. Aside from stores that sell food and medicine, everything in the city is closed. But here is a store that is selling clothing and shoes. I entered. The owner tells me that yesterday was the first day they had opened since February 24. "We'll see what happens," they say. I buy a pair of colorful Tommy Hilfiger sandals. I have absolutely nowhere to wear such sandals, but I really wanted to buy something from them. The same day I bought the sandals, in a neighborhood nearby a Russian rocket killed a 13-year-old boy at a bus stop.

And every day it is like this. You live, you eat something, you go to a restaurant, you go about your business—because you are alive, for now.

Press crew with tack medic Oleksiy Kushner. Near Bakhmut in the Donetsk region. 2022. Photograph by Oleksiy Kushner.

Later, I had a phone call with an editor from one of the big global media companies. He knows that I just returned from the front. But he starts the conversation with small talk. He is calling from London. He tells me that it's very hot in London. "Did you see news about this?" he says. "There's a heat wave now in Europe. It's terrible what's happening."

I think of the road from the front to the hotel where I'm taking this call. Holes from missiles, a blown-up bridge, burned-down village houses, dogs that wander because the owners either left or died. How can I keep up a conversation about the heat in London? Near Kharkiv there is also a heat wave and yet at the same time, grenades are flying, a tank fires and a mine-thrower, and even planes are bombing. I have enough news here without the London heat wave.

There is a video going around on social media of a Russian mercenary cutting off the genitalia of a Ukrainian prisoner of war with a box cutter. That night, I could not sleep.

My 57-year-old father-in-law was mobilized into the armed forces. Right now on the front, a dozen acquaintances and some friends are fighting. I have buried five close friends during the first six months of the war. Other friends are in captivity. I haven't had any news from them for a few months. Every morning after watching the news, where there is shelling overnight, my first thought is: how many of us were killed? I write to all my close friends on the front.

Hi, how are you?

I am just waiting for them to say "okay."

Then I kiss my son and go to make breakfast and prepare for the next trip to the front. ❋

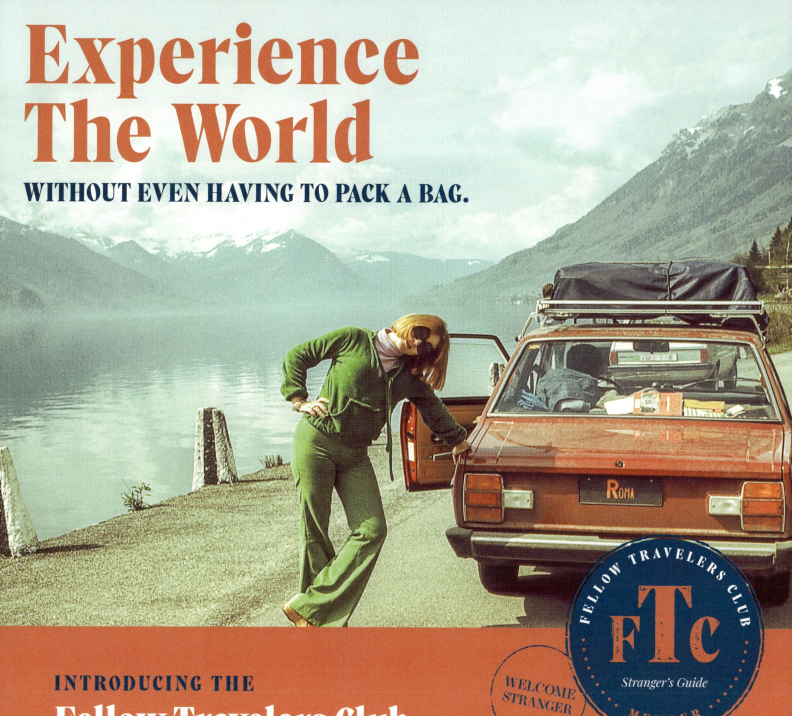

Experience The World

WITHOUT EVEN HAVING TO PACK A BAG.

INTRODUCING THE

Fellow Travelers Club

A club for those who travel the boulevards and the back alleys.

Our *Fellow Travelers Club* is for those with a sense of global curiosity and wanderlust. Our members receive a quarterly box containing our latest guide along with internationally curated food and household goods—the kinds of items you only stumble across as you explore the little store in the side alley or a local pharmacy's best-loved products.

Support journalists around the world—and get access to events, items and perks carefully curated for cosmopolitan sophisticates like yourself!

Visit strangersguide.com/subscribe to join today.

Malanka
Vasylyna Vrublevska

NEW YEAR MEANS A UNIQUE FESTIVAL in Ukraine: costumes of straw and colorful flowers; makeup to turn faces ghostly white with ruby red lips and cheeks; bear and goat costumes; masked men on horseback; dancing and carnival processions. Known as Malanka, this festival is one of the oldest in Eastern Slavic culture and traces its roots to pagan mythology. The festival takes place on January 13th, New Year's Eve, according to the Julian calendar.

Malanka is, according to ancient folklore, Mother Earth's daughter, and after she is captured by the devil, the world is devoid of Spring. But after she is released from his evil clutches, she returns so the Earth can live again. To celebrate the earth's rebirth, villagers across the country dress in elaborate costumes, prepare feasts and go from door to door singing songs. Vasylyna Vrublevska's photos allow us to celebrate with them.

The Dark Side of the Moon

In response to war, a writer abandons the Russian language.

Volodymyr Rafeenko

TRANSLATED BY
Oleksandr Frazé-Frazénko

Language is the house of being. This famous expression belongs to the German philosopher Martin Heidegger. No matter how we treat or condemn him and his ideological preferences, this man was right when he said so. Indeed, language, if it does not form a being, determines a certain range of human perceptions of this boundless world. What you are able to name, you are certainly able to see. What you can see, you have a chance to understand.

The unconditional correlation between being and language is comprehensible. What is questionable is the attempt to cram the entire world, all eternity and all otherworldliness into the framework of a single language, no matter how beautiful it may be. Language is a form of consciousness, into which sometimes the bittersweet chocolate of our present is poured, and sometimes a stream of blood. Only when I frame it this way is there a chance to understand how it happened that in my fifth decade I changed my language from Russian, my mother tongue, to Ukrainian.

...

The year 2022 turned out to be deeply difficult. In January, most of the world's media, together with US intelligence, predicted a Russian invasion. In Ukraine, people reacted to this news in different ways. Some seriously prepared for this disaster. Some, like my wife and I, tried not to think about the hard things, and instead diligently turned our attention to current affairs and creative projects. Although, to be honest, my Olesya and I had been thinking about the possibility of war for the last eight years. We felt it coming. We knew for sure that it would happen.

Donetsk in winter. 2015. Photograph by Amnon Gutman.

Ukrainian soldiers walk next to destroyed Russian tanks and armored vehicles, amid Russia's invasion of Ukraine. Bucha. 2022. Photograph by Alkis Konstantinidis/Reuters.

The fact is that for my family, this war between Russia and Ukraine began not in 2022, but back in 2014. For us, it began when Russian militants entered our city of Donetsk—a provincial industrial town in eastern Ukraine. They entered and took it quickly without a fight.

Donetsk was not small. Almost a million people lived there, and, if we take into account the entire conglomerate of small towns and villages surrounding the city, the number is probably over three million. But in 2014, Russia prepared its special operation much better. And we Ukrainians were absolutely unprepared for such an outright brazen invasion. We were dumbfounded by what happened then. We could not believe what we were seeing. On the eve of the invasion, no one could seriously conceive that Russia—our "big brother" as so many people in eastern Ukraine thought of it—would invade our lands and start cutting away pieces of our territory. But it happened. This so-called "Russian Spring." This brazen invasion. This violation of international treaties and laws. This annexation by Russia of Ukrainian Crimea and a large chunk of Donbas—an industrial region of which our hometown, Donetsk, has always been a part.

...

Donetsk was a predominantly Russian-speaking city, although this had not always been the case. For the first third of the twentieth century, Ukrainian was the dominant language in these lands. But that changed after the Second World War. Workers were brought in from all over the multilingual Soviet Union to restore the coal and metallurgical industries destroyed by the war, which, together with the agricultural sector, formed the economic foundation of the region. Many more people came here on their own to hide from the Soviet punitive system. A blind eye was turned to those who took jobs in the mines, and they usually were not touched by the penal authorities. The common language for this new multi-ethnic population was Russian. And the Soviet government, for almost all the years of its existence, continued the strategy of tsarist Russia toward Ukrainians: it diligently implemented special measures to Russify the region. This strategically important industrial region had to become predominantly Russian-speaking, so that by the time of my birth the Russian language dominated in the large cities of eastern Ukraine. Anyone for whom education, a good job or career growth was important had to speak Russian.

My parents wrote, read and spoke Russian exclusively. The first book I ever read was in Russian. I studied Ukrainian in school, but I could not communicate in Ukrainian at all until 2014.

At university, I studied at the Faculty of Russian Philology. I wrote my first poems, short stories and novels exclusively in Russian and received international literary awards for them in Moscow. Until the age of 45, until the arrival of Russian "defenders" in my house, I had no idea that I would one day learn Ukrainian, that I would one day write in two languages or that one day such events would occur, after which I would forever stop communicating in the language of my first books, my first literary work, the language of my mother and father.

When Russians seized Ukrainian territories in 2014 under the guise of protecting the Russian-speaking population, it suddenly turned out that Russian militants had come to my city to "protect" me from my homeland. These were the slogans they wrapped themselves in. But I did not need to be protected! For 45 years, I had been using the Russian language exclusively in my everyday life, in my education, in my creativity, and no one had ever said a bad word to me. When I began to realize the literal meaning of those Russian slogans, the rhetoric that the Russian propaganda machine used and still uses, I was shocked. These slogans about the protection of the Russian-speaking population made me, *me*, Volodymyr Rafeenko, one of the main reasons for this war. Do you understand? The reason for the annexation of Ukrainian territories, this horror that began in my city with the arrival of these "defenders." That is, the very cause of this tragedy that was playing out in the city of my childhood was none other than myself. And I was guilty, in fact, only in that I had spoken and written Russian since childhood.

Of course, these armed people who occupied the center of my city in early July 2014 were not at all actually interested in the fate of the Russian-speaking population of Ukraine. In fact, they did not care about it at all. They were just doing their dirty work for a bit of money. The propaganda machine of Russia, inventing these slogans, had in mind not so much us, the inhabitants of the region, but Europe, the United States and the Western world. At that time, my family and I lived in the very center of Donetsk, 20 meters from the boulevard named after the Russian poet Pushkin. In the days of the so-called "Russian Spring," literally under our windows, long bus convoys stopped, bringing hundreds of Russians from Russia, who then went to the square in front of the building of the regional state administration and there, in front of the cameras of Russian TV channels, play-acted the enthusiasm and joy of the "local population." It was bad, but well-paid theater.

As we looked at all this, we slowly realized the depth of the abyss to which our city was heading—and us along with it. Much later, we learned that a developed network of Russian subversive groups was operating in Donetsk in early 2014. That this spring had been prepared for a long time and thoughtfully. For years before that, Russians had been recruiting and attracting the heads of Donetsk law enforcement agencies to their side. At the beginning of this special operation, they were at least loyal to the systematic seizure of the city, sabotaged security measures, and allowed agents of influence and officers of the Russian special services to do their job. In that spring, people who came to pro-Ukrainian rallies with slogans of Ukrainian unity were exposed to terrible danger. There was simply no one to protect the civilian population in the city.

That year, spring turned out to be blooming and wet. Almost every day, there were showers, through which hot orange lightning struck and struck again over the city. The greenery was incredibly abundant. The smell of apricots made my head spin. The smell of doom and flowering trees floated over Donetsk. We hoped that Kyiv would send military and police units to Donetsk to clear the city of Russian mercenaries. But our hopes were not to be fulfilled.

...

By July, it became clear that the "Russian Spring" had turned into an open occupation. There was simply no chance for Ukraine to return to the region in the near future. The situation had gone too far. My family and I had to decide what to do.

To be honest, we did not hesitate for long. We saw the faces of those who came to our city with weapons. We heard what they were talking about. We clearly understood that if we stayed in the city, with our pro-Ukrainian views, we would not survive.

We left everything: our homes, our friends, our parents who did not want to leave because they still had sentiments about Russia as a "brotherly country." The parks and rivers, the familiar streets from childhood. The vast and boundless Donetsk steppe, to which I know nothing that compares. And the great Ukrainian sun that rose every day over the steppe,

FALSE FRIENDS: RUSSIAN & UKRAINIAN LANGUAGES

Ukrainian and Russian share between 55% & 62% of their vocabulary. *(English and Dutch share roughly the same percent).*

A Ukrainian with no knowledge of Russian would understand about **5 OUT OF 8 WORDS.**

In daily communication:
51% use only Ukrainian
33% use both languages
15% use only Russian
(according to recent polls)

FIRST LANGUAGES OF UKRAINIANS IN 2001 *(most recent census):*

UKRAINIAN: 68%   **RUSSIAN: 30%**

FIRST LANGUAGES IN 2022 *(recent poll):*

UKRAINIAN: 80%   **RUSSIAN: 16%**

Ukrainian became the country's official language in 1989.

Both languages use the Cyrillic alphabet, but:

• *4 Ukrainian letters are not used in Russian*
(Ґ, Є, І, Ї)

• *4 Russian letters are not used in Ukrainian*
(Ё, Ъ, Ы, Э)

• *2 letters look the same but sound different*
(Е, И)

"My own mother tongue is Russian. But the war makes us want to become more Ukrainian. We don't want to have anything in common with the Russians who are killing us." —*Odesa native Oleksandr Babich*

Ukrainian broadcasts in the Ukrainian language:
TV, 2011: 22.2%
TV, 2019: 92%
RADIO, 2011: 4.6%
RADIO, 2019: 57%

AN 1863 ORDER BY THE RUSSIAN EMPIRE PROHIBITED PUBLICATIONS IN THE UKRAINIAN LANGUAGE.

Under the Russian Empire and the Soviet Union, schools taught in Russian.

RUSSIAN AND UKRAINIAN HAVE A LOT OF "FALSE FRIENDS"—WORDS THAT LOOK ALIKE BUT HAVE DIFFERENT MEANINGS. EXAMPLES:

"горілка" in Ukrainian means *vodka*; in Russian "горелка" means *burner*.
"рожа" in Ukrainian is a type of plant; in Russian, it means *mug*, as in an ugly face.

---

full of grasses and springs, and floated there all day to the west over the sown fields, fertile gardens, over all this life that was already doomed to death. In the train from Donetsk to Kyiv, I looked at the moon rolling over our steppe and thought that it, like me, also has two sides that never meet: the side that everyone sees and the one that is always hidden from view. In my soul, the clear and open side has always been the Russian language. It was natural to speak and write Russian in my Russian-speaking family, in my Russian-speaking region. But there was also a side that remained invisible for many years. My grandmother's, my father's and my mother's native language was Ukrainian. And if the first books I read were in Russian, the first folk tales I listened to were in Ukrainian. My late grandmother, Marfa Oleksandrivna, told them to me in my childhood. It was the custom in my family to talk about our strange situation with language, but after everything that happened, I realized that I had to do something.

So on that train, on that sleepless night, when I was leaving my city forever, I promised myself that I would learn Ukrainian, that I would speak and write in this language. And I would do it so that everyone who has eyes can see that for a Ukrainian, even if he was born in Donbas, the Ukrainian language is not a problem. Because every new language you master is happiness and joy. A new language is a new key to the formation of the ontology of one's life.

I cannot say that it was easy for me to fulfill the promises I made to myself on that night in 2014. It took me several years to master just the most conversational aspects of the language. Three more years and I began to write my first novel in Ukrainian. I wrote and, at the same time, continued to study the language. I read in Ukrainian, listened to songs and communicated in Ukrainian as best I could. It took another three years to finish the novel. But, as it seemed to me, those years were not in vain. The novel, *Mondegreen: Songs about Death and Love,* was first published in Ukraine. And before the war, it was translated and published in English by the Ukrainian Institute of Harvard University and translated by Mark Andryczyk.

I made a decision from that day on to write in two languages: one novel in Ukrainian, then one in Russian. And so on until my death. After *Mondegreen* I worked on a novel in Russian for almost three years. I had planned to finish it in the winter of 2022, but then the full-scale Russian invasion began. After that, returning to it became impossible for me.

...

In early 2022, my wife and I were living in a friend's country house 30 kilometers from Kyiv, in a small country village located in the forest on the shore of the large, beautiful Lake Gloria, geographically approximately between Bucha and Borodyanka (you may have already heard these names in connection with the war). On February 24, year after year, my wife and I celebrate our wedding anniversary. This year we decided not to go anywhere, as the Covid times made traveling difficult. So we chose to celebrate our family holiday at home.

But on the morning of February 24, the day of our anniversary, Russia invaded Ukraine. Rockets attacked. Russian tank columns moved on Kyiv along the roads where we stood. As early as nine o'clock in the morning, there were battles raging between us and the capital. Heavy artillery was firing. It was so loud that the house was shaking and the doors swung open by themselves.

In a matter of days, there was no electricity, no mobile communication, no water and no internet. All communication stopped. Shops and pharmacies closed. There was no way to get anywhere. All roads around us were clogged with Russian military equipment, which the armed forces of Ukraine were diligently destroying. But the terrible truth was that we once again found ourselves in occupied territories. And there was no chance for rescue.

We lived under occupation for more than a month. I will not describe all the horrors of that time. Russians raged through the nearby villages. They killed civilians. They mocked the Ukrainian troops by placing their tanks between the huts of the village and firing from there, knowing full well that our people would not be able to shoot back at them without risking hitting the house. They did not come to our dacha cooperative in these first weeks of the war, because strategically, it was not a good location for them. We had neither electricity nor water, and the Russians, of course, needed comfort. We may also have been spared by the fact that, on the map, this series of summer cottages along the lake was marked only as "Nearby Gardens." It was not explained on the map what these "Nearby Gardens" were, so it is quite possible that the Russians thought that there were no people there, only gardens or woods. But whatever the reason, frankly speaking, I was sure that my wife and I would not survive if we stayed. We were lucky. A friend in Kyiv found help connecting us with volunteers who risked their lives to take us in their cars to Ukrainian territory. We drove slowly from one Russian checkpoint to another. As we passed by, I looked at the tanks stationed between the village houses, and at the Russian soldiers checking our cars, and I thought about the impossibility of ever returning to the Russian language, at least in my work.

Finally, the string of Russian checkpoints ended, and our Ukrainian ones began. The road to Kyiv was clear, and we were driving steadily toward the moon as it came out from behind the trees. The sun had not yet set, but the moon had already risen. I looked at it and realized that I would never be able to write in Russian again. The language of murderers, rapists and thieves. I realized that my Russian language was completely moving to the dark side of the moon, that is, entering the shadow in which my Ukrainian language had been for almost 50 years. I also thought about my family, about old family stories and about the fact that life is a very strange and unpredictable thing.

...

I wrote a play about the weeks we spent under occupation, as well as a whole number of essays for various newspapers and magazines, mostly European. All this time, I have been writing almost exclusively in Ukrainian. I think in Ukrainian. From the dark side of the moon, sometimes I can hear the Russian-speaking voices of my soul, but my native language slowly begins to rest in me. She is perhaps present somewhere in my consciousness, but increasingly she recedes into the shadows.

The moon never shows us its dark side. The truth is that, for the moon, there is neither tragedy or existential tension. Nor does it feel the pain that is always with me now. ❃

HARDLY EVER OTHERWISE
Maria Matos, 2007 | translated by Yuri Tkacz

Something had come over Vasylyna when Andriyko was about to be conceived. She had raced about after Kyrylo like an untouched virgin. Despite already having two children, she felt heady, just as she had once felt in her youth after partaking of too much green poppy-head juice in an effort to extinguish the pain of several days of toothache.

Oh, back then she had quelled her impatience for her husband's caresses wherever she could: in the pastures, in the sheep pens, in the maize fields, on the hay. She trembled like a leaf and spread out before him like mown grass. Kyrylo only needed to give her a sign, to squeeze his elbow and seek out a place with his eyes where they could press against each other. If the Earth had caved in under them or the end of the world had come, Vasylyna wouldn't have noticed a thing.

It all passed after she had given birth. It was as if that sweet and foolish itch had never even existed. She would lie down beside her husband, and slowly they would go about their usual perennial business, then turn over back to back—and lay like dead bodies until morning, without even twitching at the break of day.

Vasylyna loved Andriy more than she loved her other sons. She hadn't breastfed any of the others until they were three years old, as she had Andriy. Or else, as she went about her duties in the house, she would suddenly stop and silently stroke the boy's head, or else land a kiss on his ear, so that no one else would see.

If any job was difficult, it would sooner fall to Dmytryk's lot to do it, while Andriy was told to peel potatoes or to go off and pick beet tops for the pigs, so that he would not be exhausted. She wanted her favoured son to retain his male virility and a desire for women, just like his father.

She had pampered him enough. Now Nastunia looked after Andriychyk and molly-coddled him instead of his mother, compensating for the tatty dowry with which she had arrived with caresses and lovemaking. As if there had been no rich farmer's daughter in Tysova Rivnia for Andriy, he had brought this perforated piece of merchandise all the way from Pidzakharychi. All she had were breasts like those of a wet nurse and a plait dangling down to her ankles.

And now only her breasts, sucked dry by her children, were dangling down. Her plait, cut off at the wedding, lay in a chest in the storehouse. There was no time to play with the plait—she had to be a farmer's wife, even though there was precious little to farm.

Artwork by Aid2Art artists Svetlana Grib (left) & Helen Baranovska (pages 70-73).
Read more about Aid2Art on pages 104 through 109.

DEPECHE MODE
Serhiy Zhadan, 2004 | translated 2013 by Myroslav Shkandrij

I have quite a few friends, you can't really call us a group, we're more a kind of friendly collection of conmen out to sucker every recruiter and employer, we live in several adjoining rooms on the same floor, sleep wherever there's room, I don't even know everyone, there's only one real friend here—Vasia the Communist—the rest are more or less transients, although they're also our friends, they appear and disappear, sometimes there can be up to ten of them on our floor, at other times I wander around the corridors by myself for days, cimb onto the roof and look around. We are all 18 or 19, most of my friends have been thrown out of school, they are now either unemployed or spend their time doing useless things…

Further down the corridor, somewhere in its depth lives Cocoa the Donbas intellectual. That is, his mother works in the library of one of the mines. Cocoa is portly and we don't like him, but he's still drawn to us, well, in general he doesn't really have any alternatives, who's going to spend time with a Donbas intellectual. Although he does have some other acquaintances in the city besides us, some musicians, obviously dandies like Cocoa, and after visiting them he crawls home on all fours completely plastered on port wine, and collapses into sleep. Cocoa has a sand-colored suit in which he looks like a total nerd, he just about never takes it off, almost takes it into the shower with him too; when he fills himself with port wine he falls into bed in this suit, it turns out to be a multi-functional thing, this costume of a Donbas intellectual. When he wakes up, Cocoa comes to the kitchen and observes who is preparing what, sniffs the processed foods, and chats about various subjects—sober, portly, in his crumpled dandy costume.

Further down the corridor, somewhere in that labyrinth, lives Sailor, a solitary guy with a torn right ear, he says that a dog bit it off—Pavlov? someone is always sure to ask by way of a joke. Sailor is either God-fearing or maybe just a bit nerdy, I don't even know how to explain it, for example he only washes at night, says he doesn't want to be disturbed—disturbed from doing what? I ask him all the time, Sailor blushes but continues to wash only at night, that's how he is.

Among the others one could perhaps mention Carburetor, that's right, Sasha Carburetor, my good friend, Sasha arrived from some place along the border, though this border is everywhere around us, Sasha in fact came in defiance of his parents' wishes, it turns out that such things do indeed

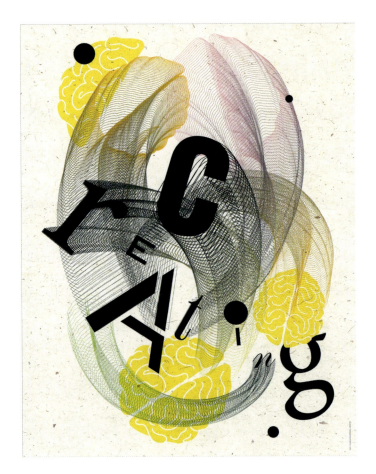

happen, his mother and stepfather are still at home; Sasha finished driver education courses, has a real driver's license, and hopes to start a trucking operation some day, to buy a hearse or something and to transport, say, furniture, he's passionate about technology, if you understand what I mean. One time he even bought himself a textbook with diagrams and descriptions of automobiles and tried to make sense of it all. He began, as you can probably guess, with the carburetor. After this the textbooks disappeared, I figure someone just sold them for alcohol, why not put them to good use. Overall, Carburetor has this capacity for stepping into shit that isn't meant for him.

As for the others, I don't even know them very well myself, various comic book heroes appear from time to time, but to keep track of them all and why they have appeared in our lives is pretty hard to do. Let's say some Ivanenko appears, a curious type, not to say fucked-up, and basically, that's about all that can be said about him. That's all there is.

A nice, eternally hungry crew, held together by no one knows what, because in principle everyone has issues with everyone else, but this is still no reason to avoid healthy interaction. We have nothing to do for the most part, although everyone has his own relations with reality, at our age these come down to some sort of simple whims and desires—to get laid, or something, I don't know what else there is. Women ignore us, even the prostitutes on the ring-road, we occasionally go over to look at the prostitutes, sort of an excursion to see the free attractions, of course we have no money, so we just hang out with them, bum some cigarettes, share various life stories, in a word we get in their way while they're trying to earn prostitution's hard bread. However, they treat us well, out there on the ring-road they're not particularly useful to anybody, just like us, and just like us they don't have enough money or societal love, both they and we have to live through the torrents of rain this summer in an empty Kharkiv suburb overgrown with grass and plastered with advertisements, this fantastic city, these fantastic prostitutes, this fantastic life. We don't practice homosexuality, though everything is leading us in that direction.

FIELDWORK IN UKRAINIAN SEX

Oksana Zabuzhko, 1996 | translated by Halyna Hyrn

And you also might say—appearing with a lecture at some American university, or at the "triple-A, double-S" conference, or at the Kennan Institute in Washington, or wherever else the ill wind blows you, an honorarium of a hundred, two hundred bucks max, plus travel costs—and thank you very much, you're not Yevtushenko or Tatiana Tolstaya to get thousands for each appearance, and who the hell are you anyway, backwater Ukrainian from the Khrushchev communal housing projects that you've been trying to break out of your whole damn life to no avail, Cinderella who crosses the ocean to grouse over dinner at Sheffield's with a pair Nobel prize winners (radiating in all directions, juggling four languages at once across the table) about the intellectual bankruptcy of contemporary civilization, after which you return to your six-square-meter Kyiv kitchen to fight with your mother and be humiliated by having to explain to various editors that "my homeland will be where I am" does not at all mean *ubi bene, ibi patria*—not least because with this fucking patria it will never and nowhere be *bene* for you, neither at Sheffield's, nor at Tiffany's, nor in Hawaii, nor Florida—because your homeland is not simply the land of your birth, a true homeland is the country that can *kill* you—even at a distance, the same

way a mother slowly but inexorably kills an adult child by holding it near, shackling its every move and thought with her burdensome presence—ah, to make a long story short, the topic of my lecture today, ladies and gentlemen, is, as noted in the program, "Fieldwork in Ukrainian Sex," and before I begin I would like to thank all of you, present here and absent, for the completely unjustified attention you have given my country and my humble persona—because if there's one thing that we haven't been spoiled by yet it's attention: to put it bluntly, we've been lying there dying, unnoticed by bloody anybody (and I'm still in a rather privileged position here, because if I were to really have the guts to say fuck it and pour the rest of those tablets in the orange bottle down my throat, my body would be found relatively soon, I'd say, probably within three days: Chris, the departmental secretary, will call if I don't show up for class, therefore, it would be a crime to complain, the spider web-thin thread, slight as it is, still hangs there and I could pull on it to let the world know about my next, this time my final, departure, I do have it—and if something were to happen with that man in the Pennsylvania wilderness—although I really doubt that anything should happen to him, he'd never do it himself, too much rage for this kind of business—then he's got Mark and Rosie checking in on him daily)—so, ladies and gentlemen, please do not be in a hurry to qualify the presented case of love here as pathological, because the speaker has not yet stated what is most important—the main point, ladies and gentlemen, lies in the fact that in the research subject's life this was her first *Ukrainian* man. Honestly—the first.

The first one *ready-made*—whom she did **not** have to teach Ukrainian, to drag book after book from her personal library out on dates with him just to broaden the common internal space on which to build a relationship (Lypynsky, Hrushevsky, and he hadn't heard of Horska either, nor Svitlychny, his idea of the 1960s dissident movement was completely different, good, I'll bring it for you tomorrow!), or if in bed after lovemaking you inadvertently quote "nor dreams' abode—the sacred home," you have to immediately launch into a half-hour commentary on the life and works of the author—oh, there was this writer in Western Ukraine in the 1930s—and that's the way it was your whole damned life!—professional Ukrainianizer, like growing a whole new organ for each of them, and if some day our independent, or rather not-yet-dead country, if it doesn't die by then, should institute some special award—for the highest number of Ukrainianized bed spaces, you'd surely sock it to them with your grand list of conversions!—but this was the first man from *your world*, the first with whom you could exchange not merely words, but simultaneously the entire boundlessness of shimmering secret treasure troves, reflections from inside the deepest wells that are revealed by those words, and therefore it was as easy to talk as to breathe and to dream, and that's why the conversation was drunk eagerly with parched, dry lips, the intoxication ever more dizzying, ah, this never-before experienced total freedom to be yourself, this four-hands piano playing, at last, across the entire keyboard, inspiration and improvisation, so many sparks, laughter, and energy suddenly released, when each note—ironic hint, nuance, wit, touch—resonates at once, picked up by your interlocutor, somersaults in the air for no reason other than excess of strength, a casual touch of the knee—a little closer: may I? and now a little more ambiguous, more risky, and now—up close and personal, and finally, turning off the car engine (because you did end up getting into that stupid car of his after all—after visiting his studio, after you saw with your own eyes *who* he was)—an abrupt switch to a different language: lips, tongue, hands—and you, leaning back with a moan, *"Let's go to your place…To the studio…"*—a language that drastically shortened your path toward one another, you recognized him: he's one of yours, yours—in everything, a beast of the same species!—and in that language there was everything, everything of which there would later be nothing between you in bed.

VOICES FROM CHERNOBYL: THE ORAL HISTORY OF A NUCLEAR DISASTER

Svetlana Alexievich, 1997 | translated 2005 by Keith Gessen

So what is Chernobyl? A lot of military hardware and soldiers. Wash posts. A real military situation. They placed us in tents, ten men to a tent. Some of us had kids at home, some had pregnant wives, others were in between apartments. But nobody complained. If we had to do it, we had to do it. The motherland called and we went. That's just how we are.

There were enormous piles of empty tin cans around the tents. The military depots have a special supply in case of war. The cans were from canned meat, pearl buckwheat, sprats. There were groups of cats all around, they were like flies. The villages had been emptied—you'd hear a gate open and turn around expecting a person, and instead there'd be a cat walking out.

We dug up the diseased top layer of soil, loaded it into automobiles and took it to waste burial sites. I thought that a waste burial site was a complex, engineered construction, but

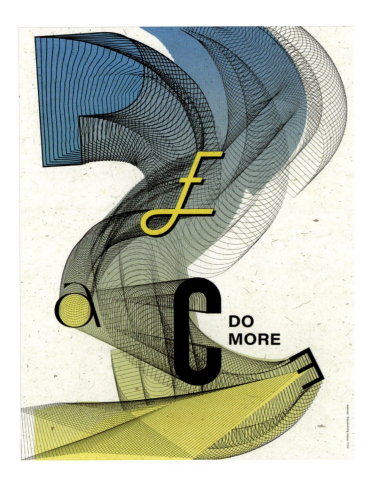

it turned out to be an ordinary pit. We picked up the earth and rolled it, like big rugs. We'd pick up the whole green mass of it, with grass, flowers, roots. And bugs, and spiders, worms. It was work for madmen. You can't just pick up the whole earth, take off everything living. If we weren't drinking like crazy every night, I doubt we'd have been able to take it. Our psyches would have broken down. We created hundreds of kilometers of torn-up, fallow earth. The houses, barns, trees, highways, kindergartens, wells—they all remained there, naked. In the morning you'd wake up, you need to shave, but you're afraid to look in the mirror and see your own face. Because you're getting all sorts of thoughts. It's hard to imagine people moving back to live there again. But we changed the slate, we changed the roofs on houses. Everyone understood that this was useless work, and there were thousands of us. Every morning we'd get up and do it again. We'd meet an illiterate old man: "Ah, quit this silly work, boys. Have a seat at the table, eat with us." The wind would be blowing, the clouds floating. The reactor wasn't even shut down. We'd take off a layer of earth and come back in a week and start over again. But there was nothing left to take off—just some sand that had drifted in. The one thing we did that made sense to me was when some helicopters sprayed a special mixture that created a polymer film that kept the light-moving bottom-soil from moving. That I understood. But we kept digging, and digging.

The villages were evacuated, but some still had old men in them. To walk into an old peasant hut and sit down to dinner—just the ritual of it—a half hour of normal life. Although you couldn't eat anything, it wasn't allowed. But I so wanted to sit at the table, in an old peasant hut.

After we were done the only thing left were the pits. They were going to fill them with concrete plates and surround them with barbed wire, supposedly. They left the dump trucks, cargo trucks, and cranes they'd been using there, since metal absorbs radiation in its own way. I've been told that all that stuff has since disappeared, that is, been stolen. I believe it. Anything is possible here now.

One time we had an alarm: the dosimetrists discovered that our cafeteria had been put in a spot where the radiation was higher than where we went to work. We'd already been there two months by then. That's just how we are. The cafeteria was just a bunch of posts and these had boards nailed to them at chest height. We ate standing up. We washed ourselves from barrels filled with water. Our toilet was a long pit in a clear field. We had shovels in our hands, and not far off was the reactor.

After two months we began to understand things a little. People started saying: "This isn't a suicide mission. We've been here two months—that's enough. They should bring in others now." Major-General Antoshkin had a talk with us. He was very honest. "It's not advantageous for us to bring in a new shift. We've already given you three sets of clothing. And you're used to the place. To bring in new men would be expensive and complicated." With an emphasis on our being heroes. Once a week someone who was digging really well would receive a certificate of merit before all the other men. The Soviet Union's best grave digger. It was crazy.

These empty villages—just cats and chickens. You walk into a barn, it's filled with eggs. We'd fry them. Soldiers are ready for anything. We'd catch a chicken, put it on the fire, wash it down with a bottle of homemade vodka. We'd put away a three-liter bottle of that stuff every night in the tent. Someone'd be playing chess, another guy was on his guitar. A person can get used to anything. One guy would get drunk and fall down on his bed to sleep, other guys wanted to yell and fight. Two of them got drunk and went for a drive and crashed. They got them out from under the crushed metal with the jaws of life. I saved myself by writing long letters home and keeping a diary. The head of the political

department noticed, he kept asking me what I was writing, where was I keeping it? He got my neighbor to spy on me, but the guy warned me. "What are you writing?" "My dissertation." He laughs. "All right, that's what I'll tell the colonel. But you should hide that stuff." They were good guys. I already said, there wasn't a single whiner in the bunch. Not a single coward. Believe me: no one will ever defeat us. Ever! The officers never left their tents. They'd walk around in slippers all day, drinking. Who cares? We did our digging. Let the officers get another star on their shoulder. Who cares? That's the sort of people we have in this country.

LIFE WENT ON ANYWAY

Oleg Sentsov, 2019 | translated by Uilleam Blacker

I had a grandmother and I didn't like her. It happens.

•••

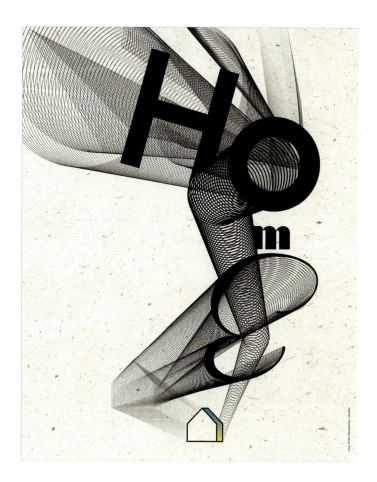

It also might happen that you're born a woman, you live in a small village, you work your whole life, of your four children only one survives, your husband eventually leaves you for another woman, and you're left alone. Okay, not entirely alone—with a child. The child then grows up, goes off to study, then to the army, then gets married, and goes to live far away and forever. And then you're left entirely entirely alone. I can't imagine how all this would feel, and I don't want to.

•••

Your son visits very rarely, brings a grandson or granddaughter. But their visits are short and reluctant. Then you hit seventy, your son comes to visit for the last time, you sell the old wooden house and move in with him, into a stone house far away. Apart from your son, your grandson, your granddaughter, and your son's wife live there. They're not pleased to have you there. They're not mean to you, they put up with you, it's called "caring for an elderly parent."

The room is separate and new, but the things in it are all old, from the wooden house. The room quickly absorbs the smell of old age. They bring you your pension on time, nobody wants to take it away from you, they never even ask, and you can spend it however you like. How you like is usually on grocery shopping, sometimes you give some to your son's wife—there's never enough money in any family and this family is no exception. The rest goes into your savings book, like it should. You do it, the family you live with does it. That's the best way, it's safer.

Every other day they bring you newspapers, you can read them. Sometimes they invite you to come and watch television in the living room. They make food for you regularly. On Saturday, they go to the bathhouse and "do you need anything washed?" In the evening you can pray, kneeling in your old nightgown. At night, you urinate into a one-liter jar—it's too cold and dark to go to the outside toilet. You can also write letters to grandmas just like you who live far away and sometimes get replies. As the years pass, the letters are sent and received less and less frequently.

All of these activities take up most of your time. The rest of the time you can sit in your room and look out the window. You can see everything: who comes, who goes, who came through the gate from that direction, who left in that direction, who walked along the street, who drove along it. True, you can't see the street so well, you have a better view of the gate, but the window is big, with curtains. You can hide behind them sometimes, so nobody can see that you're watching everybody.

An Ultra orthodox Jewish man talks with World War II veteran. Uman. 2008. Photograph by Konstantin Chernichkin/Reuters.

At the Limits of Nationalism

Confronting Ukraine's past to imagine its future

David Klion

No one spoke of Ukrainian nationality before the nineteenth century. Nor did a state named Ukraine exist before the twentieth. Ukraine isn't very different from its Eastern European neighbors in this regard; modern nations, by and large, were dreamt up by nineteenth century intellectuals and realized by twentieth century statesmen and soldiers, all of whom selectively cited diverse and often contradictory historical forces and figures to justify their immediate political aims. Nationality is always constructed, and nations—as the Anglo-Irish historian Benedict Anderson famously argued—are "imagined communities" projected back into the past to serve present-day agendas. In the case of Ukraine, this meant connecting the dots between ancient Greek colonists, Sarmatian tribes, Christian Slavs of Medieval Kyivan Rus, Orthodox peasants of the Polish-Lithuanian Commonwealth's eastern frontiers, seventeenth century Cossacks, Ruthenians of Habsburg Galicia and Bukovyna, the "Little Russians" of Romanov Russia and not-always-welcome Jews and Crimean Tatars. All of these histories and communities were united to produce a coherent national narrative supporting the existence of an independent Ukrainian nation-state—the state whose legitimacy Vladimir Putin called into question when justifying Russia's invasion of Ukraine in 2022.

The global face of Ukraine's resistance to Russia's invasion has been, of course, that of President Volodymyr Zelensky. His Jewish background and native fluency in Russian have been widely cited as refutations of Putin's central premise—that Ukraine is controlled by a fascist junta brought to power in a 2014 coup backed by the United States and its NATO allies, and that Russia is committed to "denazification" and to defending the rights of Ukraine's allegedly oppressed Russian-speaking population. "How could I be a Nazi?" Zelensky asked rhetorically in a plea for peace just before the invasion. A comedian and actor by training, Zelensky has been uniquely positioned to present Ukraine to the Western powers whose military and financial backing it depends on as a familiar, appealing and essentially liberal country fighting for its sovereignty against Putin's authoritarian empire. In this context, Zelensky's Jewishness has played a key role in neutralizing Ukraine's historical reputation for antisemitism. Without Zelensky, it is difficult to imagine the blue and gold banner of Ukraine becoming a fixture in progressive American neighborhoods, displayed alongside Black Lives Matter signs and intersectional rainbow flags.

Somehow, a nation that reveres the legacy of the Cossacks has become identified around the world with Western democratic values. How that pairing became possible, and whether it's sustainable, could help determine whether Ukraine prevails in its war with Russia—and more fundamentally, whether pluralism and nationalism can coexist anywhere. The latter is a question the entire world has a stake in, and answering it will require an honest engagement with some of the most controversial symbols of Ukraine's national identity.

• • •

One of the most prominent landmarks in Kyiv is an equestrian statue of Bohdan Khmelnytsky that was erected in 1888 in Sophia Square, between the similarly iconic Sophia Cathedral and St. Michael's Monastery. The seventeenth century Cossack leader is also depicted on the five-hryvnia note, worth roughly 15 cents. Cities and streets throughout Ukraine bear Khmelnytsky's name, as does a bridge in Moscow near the railway station to Kyiv. So too does a military honor that Zelensky has awarded to numerous soldiers who have resisted Russia's invasion.

Every nation has its heroes, but few are as polarizing as Khmelnytsky. To Poles and Ashkenazi Jews throughout the global diaspora, Khmelnytsky, the founder of the Cossack state known as the Hetmanate, is often grouped with Hitler and Stalin as one of history's most reviled mass murderers. The Cossack Uprising he led in 1648, generally considered a key moment in the founding of the modern Ukrainian nation, was an uprising against western Ukraine's ruling Polish nobility and its de facto alliance with Jewish merchants and artisans. Recent scholarship estimates that tens of thousands of Jews were massacred by the Cossacks under Khmelnytsky's command. Even some Ukrainian nationalists—including Taras Shevchenko, the beloved national poet—have questioned Khmelnytsky's legacy, since it includes the 1654 Pereiaslav Agreement pledging the Cossacks to the service of the Russian Tsar. Khmelnytsky's defenders characterize the agreement as a pragmatic alliance intended to secure Cossack autonomy against the Poles, while Russian and Soviet historians have tended to cite it as a legal basis for the Moscow-ruled Ukraine that Russia now seeks to restore by force.

To the polonophile historian Norman Davies, Khmelnystsky "brought a murderous army of Cossacks and Tatars right up to the Vistula [and] left a swathe of butchered Catholics and Jews across Ukraine." In *The Atlantic*, David Frum writes that Khmelnytsky "murdered Polish landlords and Polish Catholic priests when he could get them, but he above all targeted Jews. He killed thousands and enslaved thousands more. Khmelnytsky's atrocities haunted Jewish memory for generations, until they were overshadowed by the even more terrible organized mass murder of the twentieth century." Leon Wieseltier recently called Khmelnytsky "one of the most reviled figures in Jewish history," responsible for "some of the most hideous atrocities in the annals of anti-Semitic violence," and said the hetman's name was "a common curse word" among the Brooklyn Jews of his childhood.

Serhii Plokhy, a Harvard scholar and bestselling author of *The Gates of Europe: A History of Ukraine*, doesn't deny any of this, but he stresses how Ukrainian historians have tended to regard Khmelnytsky: "They extolled him as the father of the nation, the liberator of his people from the Polish yoke, and the hetman who had negotiated the best possible arrangement with the tsar." In the Ukrainian national imagination, Khmelnytsky's Cossacks are less marauding killers and rapists than something akin to the mythologized American cowboys or Argentine gauchos: proud, independent horsemen defending the frontier against those who would impose imperial order upon it. To Ukrainians attempting to assert a unique national destiny, the Cossacks represent freedom from serfdom and from any kind of foreign domination; their folkways are distinctly Ukrainian and bridge the country's east-west divisions.

At the extremes, those divisions are undeniable. The westernmost parts of Ukraine were never under Russian control before the twentieth century. Rather, they were shaped by Central European influences, which explains, for instance, the prevalence of the Greek Catholic or "Uniate" Church in the west, which reconciles Orthodox Christian rites with fealty to the Vatican. By contrast, the easternmost regions, along with Crimea, were heavily settled by Russians in the nineteenth and twentieth centuries to further Tsarist and Soviet strategies of imperial and industrial development. The large middle of the country surrounding the Dnieper Valley, the Cossack heartland, is where these easy distinctions collapse, and where bilingualism is most common. Both east and west are plausibly tied to the legacy of Khmelnytsky's Hetmanate, even as they understand that legacy and its implications for present-day Ukraine in very different ways.

If the Cossacks have been broadly accepted as foundational to Ukrainian identity, the legacy of the nationalist Stepan Bandera has been far thornier. Bandera was born in Eastern Galicia in 1909, in what was then the Austro-Hungarian Empire. By the time he was nine, the empire had dissolved into multiple new or expanded nation-states, and for a brief moment, it looked as if Ukraine might be one of them. But the initial attempt to establish an independent Ukraine failed—most of its territory became a

LENINFALL

In 1991, Ukraine had **5,500 STATUES** *of Vladimir Lenin—the world's highest density*

(RUSSIA, 28X BIGGER THAN UKRAINE, HAD 7,000)

Toppling Lenin statues is called *Leninopad* (Leninfall)

FORGOTTEN BUT NOT GONE:
- Novooleksiivka converted its Lenin into Pylyp Orlykov, author of the first Ukrainian constitution.
- Cherasky's Lenin is now a Ukrainian Cossack outside a sports club.
- Artist Alexander Milov transformed one into Darth Vader. It stands in a factory courtyard in Odesa.
- A decapitated statue in Shabo was painted gold.
- Artist Yuri Didovets incorporated the Bessarabska Lenin's smashed head into an insectoid sculpture.

Some were discreetly removed; others, like the one from Bessarabska Square, Kyiv, were toppled by protesters.

THE REMAINING 1,320 WERE REMOVED AFTER A 2015 LAW MANDATED IT.

OFFICIALLY, NONE REMAIN.

Plinths in some town squares stand empty.

MANY OF THE LENINS LANGUISH IN JUNK HEAPS AND STORAGE CLOSETS.

The village of Kodaky sold its Lenin statue for roughly $5,000. The money was used to replace the school's windows.

A 2016 poll on dismantling the Lenin monuments showed:

41% FOR
48% AGAINST

---

component republic of the newly established Soviet Union, and the western region that had been Austro-Hungarian ended up in a reborn Poland. Bandera came of age in the latter, becoming involved in Ukrainian nationalism as a youth. At age 20, he joined the Organization of Ukrainian Nationalists, a far-right group founded in Vienna that was committed to establishing an independent Ukraine. Later, he became the leader of its more radical wing. After being imprisoned for life for attempting to assassinate a Polish official in 1934, Bandera was freed in September 1939 when Nazi Germany and the Soviet Union invaded Poland, with the Soviets capturing and annexing western Ukraine. He relocated to Nazi-occupied Krakow, where he began collaborating with German intelligence to support an independent, fascist Ukraine allied with Germany. During this period, Bandera's wing of the OUN committed acts of terror against Jews and Poles under German rule. However, a few months after the Nazis invaded the Soviet Union in June 1941, Bandera was arrested and sent to a German camp for political prisoners for most of the remainder of the war. He spent the postwar years in West Germany working with the CIA to subvert Soviet Ukraine and was fatally poisoned by a KGB agent in 1959.

To many Ukrainian nationalists, Bandera is remembered as a hero and a martyr. To Jews, Poles, Russians, leftists of all stripes and most historians, he was first and foremost a fascist and Nazi collaborator. Russia and its apologists today cast Ukraine's government as "Banderites," and regard all opposition to Russian domination of Ukraine as essentially fascist in character. Plokhy, in his history of Ukraine, acknowledges Bandera's fraught legacy

SOVIET CAFÉ v. ANTI-SOVIET CAFÉ

The Kyiv restaurant **KOMUNALNAYA KVARTIRA ("COMMUNAL FLAT")** recreates the atmosphere of "one big crazy family" made to live together in Soviet communal housing.

In Lviv, Kryjivka ("Secret Place" or "Bunker") mimics the secret HQ of anti-Soviet fighters of the 1940s and 50s.

Use password "SLAVA UKRAINI" (Glory to Ukraine) at the unmarked door to enter.

THE MENU LOOKS LIKE A VINTAGE NEWSPAPER.

Sports and film screenings are shown on large TVs.

FEATURED DECOR

- Mismatched chairs and "shabby-looking" tables and tablecloths
- Designer-decorated toilet seats as wall art
- Doors to various rooms in the corridor
- Bicycles attached to the wall
- Soviet-era housewares, suitcases and other artifacts

EVEN BEFORE THE WAR, RUSSIAN SPEAKERS RISKED GETTING "TAKEN HOSTAGE" AND MADE TO SING UKRAINIAN ANTHEMS.

Ordering Russian pelmeni could get a person "shot."

THE UNDERGROUND RESTAURANT IS DECORATED WITH BANNERS OF UKRAINIAN RESISTANCE HEROES, MACHINE GUNS, SHORTWAVE RADIOS AND SPENT ARTILLERY SHELLS.

WAITERS ARE DRESSED IN KHAKI, THE CROCKERY IS METAL AND THE FOOD IS SIMPLE.

Visitors can fire blanks from WWII-era weapons or spar with a Putin-faced punching bag.

---

but also notes that Bandera "had no operational control over the forces that bore his name" in waging an insurgency against the Soviet Union. His view of occupied Ukrainians who fought in Bandera's name is fundamentally tragic. "Few were happy with German rule in Ukraine, even fewer shared the Nazi ideology, and no one believed in a German future after Stalingrad and Kursk," he writes. "Apart from hard-nosed calculation, only their shared anticommunism brought the Ukrainian politicians and German authorities together."

In 2015, Ukraine's President Petro Poroshenko implemented a program of "decommunization" that has resulted in the removal of thousands of statues of Lenin and other Soviet leaders and the renaming of tens of thousands of streets. Polling a year later revealed that this policy was deeply divisive among Ukrainians, although another poll following Russia's invasion in 2022 showed much more robust support—perhaps in part driven by Putin citing "decommunization" in his speech justifying the invasion. Although the Soviet legacy is condemned by many Ukrainians—most infamously because of the Holodomor, the "death by hunger" genocide that Stalin imposed in the process of collectivizing agriculture—other Ukrainians have a more nostalgic view of the era, viewing decommunization as less a recognition of past injustice than an attack on the rights of Russian-speaking Ukrainians. After all, no one is pulling down statues of Khmelnytsky. And ultimately, as Plokhy writes, Bandera "became a symbolic leader and a proverbial father of the nation."

To Zelensky, the issue of Bandera's legacy has been tricky. In a 2019 interview, the president was asked how he reconciled his support of his predecessor Poroshenko's "decommunization" policy with the continued memorialization of Bandera. "Stepan Bandera is a hero for a certain percentage of Ukrainians, and this is normal and cool," Zelensky said. "He is one person who defended the freedom of Ukraine. But I think that when we call so many streets and bridges by the same name, this is not entirely correct." Instead, Zelensky suggested, more streets should be named for prominent artists and writers "who unite Ukraine today." A 2021 poll suggested that 32 percent of Ukrainians approve of Bandera, and Ukrainian politics have been perpetually divided over whether to recognize Bandera as an official hero of Ukraine. The pro-Western President Viktor Yushchenko attempted to do so in 2010, only to be blocked by an administrative court in the Russian-speaking city of Donetsk (which has been under the control of Russian-backed separatists since 2014). In July 2022, Zelensky fired Andriy Melnyk, Ukraine's ambassador to Germany—a country that prohibits pro-Nazi speech as penance for its central role in the Holocaust—for praising Bandera and questioning whether he was antisemitic. The firing was a case study in how delicate a position Ukraine now finds itself in—dependent on Western countries like Germany to financially support its resistance to Russia, while also relying on nationalists on the frontlines whose views play poorly in the West.

The divide over Bandera is partly ideological, with the right in favor and the left against, and partly geographic—generally speaking, he is a hero in his native western Ukraine and to many in the global Ukrainian-speaking diaspora, and a villain in the Russian-speaking east. But Bandera also has his fans in the east, especially among one faction that has become highly visible in the past eight years and that poses unresolved questions about the future of Ukrainian identity.

...

No aspect of contemporary Ukraine inspires more heated debate than the Azov Regiment, which was founded in 2014 as an independent militia, the Azov Battalion, and later incorporated into the Ukrainian National Guard. Azov was organized in response to Russia's illegal annexation of Crimea and backing of separatist republics in the eastern Donbas region—both of which followed street protesters overthrowing the unpopular but legitimately elected government of Viktor Yanukovych in what Ukrainians call the Revolution of Dignity. Consisting mainly of Russian-speaking volunteers in the Donbas region, Azov grew in part out of football hooliganism and became notorious in Russia and beyond for its frequent embrace of neo-Nazi symbols, rhetoric and ideology. Bandera is a touchstone for many Azov volunteers, some of whom go so far as to display swastikas and praise Hitler. To Western critics of Ukraine on both the left and the right, the frequent appearance of Nazi imagery in photographs of Azov volunteers has become a fixation—evidence that Russia's casus belli of "denazification" is not entirely without merit.

There's little doubt that Russian propaganda has exaggerated Azov's significance. The regiment's membership is estimated to be in the thousands across the country, concentrated in the country's embattled east, and some analysts argue that the group is far less ideologically focused than is often alleged. Far-right political parties peaked at roughly 10 percent support in Ukraine's 2012 parliamentary elections, and in 2019, a bloc of far-right parties

---

Subscribe to *Stranger's Guide* and start a new journey today.

$5 — DIGITAL ONLY
Digital-only access to our latest guides as each is released

$75 — PRINT & DIGITAL
Welcome gift
Four beautiful print guides
Digital access to our latest guides as each is released

$165 — PRINT & DIGITAL PLUS
Welcome gift
Four beautiful guides
Our complete digital library
Exclusive promotions

SUBSCRIBE TODAY AT STRANGERSGUIDE.COM/SUBSCRIBE

STRANGER'S GUIDE

Captivating stories that bring the world to you.

collectively received barely more than two percent of the vote—a smaller share than similar parties in most European countries, and insufficient to secure any seats in the Rada. Zelensky's presidential campaign that year, by contrast, won 73 percent of the vote on a vague reform platform bolstered by the comedian's performance in the TV series *Servant of the People*, a national hit (incidentally written almost entirely in Russian) in which he plays a guileless everyman who becomes president of Ukraine.

Beyond a general pledge to fight corruption, Zelensky initially seemed to offer a more conciliatory approach to Russia, appealing to a broad spectrum of Ukrainians who had grown weary of the grinding conflict in the east. In his first year in office, the new president clashed with army veterans over a proposed troop withdrawal and drew criticism from Azov's leader, Andriy Biletsky, who threatened to mobilize veterans of the Donbas war to protest Zelensky. Despite the far right's seeming electoral weakness, some analysts argue, Azov and similar militias have been able to exert political pressure on Ukraine's elected government, keeping it committed to fighting the war.

Russia's full-scale invasion of Ukraine less than three years later rendered this split moot; Zelensky, who sought peace up until the last minute and often cautioned US and British intelligence against stoking tensions with Moscow, quickly embraced his role as a wartime president and enjoyed a massive surge in popularity. In the context of a mass people's war against a foreign invader, the particular ideology of some of the citizens under arms seems less important than the urgent and just cause of national sovereignty.

...

In rallying the nation and much of the Western world in defense of Ukraine, Zelensky has relied on an inclusive, pluralistic vision of what the Ukrainian nation can be. He has lent his own considerable talents as a performer and communicator to a stunningly effective public relations blitz, at one point even participating in an Annie Leibovitz photo shoot for *Vogue* along with his wife, Olena Zelenska. Zelensky has been praised as a "Jewish hero" in *The Atlantic* and *Commentary* and credited for "comedic courage" in *The New Yorker*. Any skepticism of his political agenda, personal ethics and preparedness for national office went out the window when Zelensky declined the US government's offer for safe passage out of Kyiv; in both Ukraine and the West, he has become a living symbol of liberalism's defiance against Putin's autocratic threat. Even the left-wing publication *Jacobin*, which has frequently expressed doubts about Western support for Ukraine, published the Ukrainian socialist writer Taras Bilous criticizing Zelensky for neoliberalism but also calling him "the most moderate politician who could have come to power in Ukraine" post-2014. Ukraine could hardly have asked for a more broadly appealing face to present to the world.

In championing Zelensky's Ukraine, Western liberals believe they are backing a country that shares their values—one in which patriotic Jewish volunteers serve proudly alongside the Azov Regiment. In the early twentieth century, as Ukraine tore itself apart amid the wider Russian Civil War, soldiers on all sides committed pogroms and other atrocities against Ukraine's Jews. Today, as war rages in the country, Ukraine and Russia compete in a global propaganda contest to cast themselves as friends to the Jewish people—and their opponents as the true heirs to Nazi Germany. This shouldn't obscure the fact that actual neo-Nazis and antisemites exist in considerable numbers in both countries, but it does suggest something about the sophistication with which both governments engage with Western media narratives in 2022. As Franklin Foer writes, it "would have astounded [his] grandparents," Ukrainian Jews who narrowly escaped the Holocaust, to see a contemporary Ukraine where polls show many Ukrainians want their daughters to marry Jewish men, and where an Afghan and a Rwandan serve in parliament opposite a Jewish president—all, it should be emphasized, amid the enduring names and images of Khmelnytsky and Bandera.

The open question, then, is whether the civic nationalism that Zelensky campaigned on can be fortified by war and mass mobilization, or whether the traumas of the war and a likely imperfect resolution will end up empowering those with a narrower and uglier vision of the Ukrainian nation. This, as much as any wider geopolitical considerations, is what's at stake in Russia's war. So far, Zelensky has been the popular wartime leader of a nation more united than ever by its effort to repel Putin's invasion, but if that effort falters, this could change quickly. And Zelensky's own branding as a liberal is also at risk of being undermined by, for instance, a proposed media law intended to censor Russian propaganda that might be justified by wartime exigencies but that has run afoul of the Committee to Protect Journalists.

Of course, Ukraine is hardly the only country attempting to reconcile competing liberal and reactionary strains of its national history. For Americans to see themselves in Ukrainians is less far-fetched than it might seem. Watching Zelensky navigate these debates, I'm reminded of the image of Barack Obama, America's first Black president, standing before an Oval Office portrait of George Washington, the slaveholder whose face adorns the one-dollar bill and whose name is that of the nation's capital. A short distance from the White House, a statue of civil rights champion Martin Luther King Jr. faces a memorial to the slaveholder Thomas Jefferson. To schoolchildren touring the National Mall, both figures are now glorified Americans. Whether the United States can live up to the idealism suggested by that juxtaposition is no clearer than whether Ukraine can do the same. ✻

THE HERMIT IN THE PALACE

WHEN UKRAINE'S THEN-PRESIDENT Viktor Yanukovych fled Kyiv for Russia during the Maidan Revolution in February, 2014, he also abandoned his luxury 340-acre estate, Mezhyhirya, a sprawling site on the banks of the Dnipro River just north of Kyiv. With the president in retreat, protesters swarmed the grounds, as well as Yanukovych's private palace at its center—a grandiose home nicknamed "Honka," complete with taxidermied lions and alligators, replica suits of armor, plant pots covered in alligator skin, a $90,000 Steinway piano, gold toilets and shower fixtures and a chandelier said to be made from a quarter ton of solid silver.

One of those protesters was Petro Oliynik who had run a market stall in Lviv until the revolution. Oliynik took it upon himself to become Honka's guardian—a one-man anti-looting security force, determined to remain until the home and grounds could be protected by the state as a museum. Refusing to sleep in Yanukovych's bed, Oliynik and his girlfriend, Yulia, slept in quarters intended for kitchen staff. For years, he welcomed tourists, clad in a leather jerkin with a red-and-black flag draped over his shoulders. "If you pour blood over Ukraine's yellow and blue flag," Oliynik told one reporter, "it becomes this black and red one. This is how our flag looks in times of revolution and struggle."

Oliynik and Yulia lived off the cash visitors gave him for "tickets." His tours included showing visitors Yanukovych's fleet of classic cars, imitation Spanish galleon (with a hall inside for entertaining guests), driving range and private zoo. Also included on the tour was "Putin's guest house," a luxury guest villa on the grounds, which was always available to the Russian leader widely considered the real force behind Yanukovych's rule; the scientific lab where Yanukovych had his food tested to prevent being poisoned and, until it was stolen in 2015, a two-kilogram golden loaf of bread that had been a birthday gift from Russian oligarch Vladimir Lukyanenko. "[Yanukovych] thought he was a god," Oliynik said. Inside Honka was a billiard room, poker room, swimming pool, personal church, wellness complex (complete with tanning bed), boxing gym (Yanukovych didn't fight, but he liked to watch), four-lane bowling alley and home cinema.

Today, Oliynik has moved out, and his wish for Mezhyhirya has come true: it is open to the public as a national park.

Ukrainian Romanticism
Misha Friedman

PEOPLE GETTING BY. That's what photographer Misha Friedman wanted to chronicle in the decade between 2010 and 2020. Born in Moldova, he studied Russian politics and economics at the London School of Economics before becoming a photographer. His work with the humanitarian organization had taken him to Ukraine; his work as a photographer demanded he return. "I don't want to sound contrived," Friedman said. "I'm not a fan of statements like, 'Oh, these photographs show a whole country in limbo.' My images show people trying to get by."

One striking photograph is of a coal miner, grinning at Friedman's camera. Friedman took the photo in the Donbas region. The miners invited him to drink with them; help toast their friend's birthday with $1-a-bottle spirits. "There's this stereotype that if you work in the coal mine, everything is bad in your life; that you're suffering," Friedman said. "But they were laughing and in good spirits. To me, it was very sweet."

Another photograph of a woman holding a gun was taken at the police academy in 2015. This was post-Maidan, and Ukraine's new female police chief Khatia Dekanoidze was leading reform of the country's police service, so long criticized as one of its most oppressive institutions. Friedman said that in the past, women officers weren't allowed to patrol the streets. Now they were, and what's more, they made up a quarter of all new recruits.

Another image shows a glowing orb hovering above an industrial landscape at night. Friedman said a Ukrainian oligarch had become mesmerized by an installation he'd seen by Icelandic-Danish artist Olafur Eliasson in which a similar orb had illuminated a darkened gallery space. "One of Ukraine's richest men wanted that rising sun for himself so he commissioned Olafur to construct something similar outside his pipe factory in Dnipro."

"There's a reason journalists are attracted to Ukraine," Friedman said. "I was last there in 2021. I want to go back. There are so many stories to be told."

The Broken Yoke

Emerging from boxing's "Soviet School"

Andrii Rozanov

TRANSLATED BY
Olena Jennings

The myth of the Soviet boxer is one known around the world: think of the monotonous, brute strength of Ivan Drago, Rocky's nemesis in *Rocky IV*. He's a machine, throwing relentless punches, but fighting with little character or style. For decades, as a part of the Soviet athletic system, Ukrainian fighters were funneled into a pipeline that produced a similarly bland style of boxing. But, Ukrainian athletes pushed against the mold, stylistically and politically, asserting their independence on several levels.

Once free of the USSR, Ukraine instantly became a significant force in the boxing world. In the three decades since Ukraine's independence, Ukrainian boxing has continued to define itself as a unique counterpoint to the Soviet style from which it emerged. Several generations of fighters—starting with the Klitschko brothers and their training under the Soviet system, then evolving into the unique styles of Lomachenko and Usyk, and moving onto the individualized style of today's athletes—chart a dynamic path for boxing in Ukraine. It follows a trajectory similar to the new nation itself: shaking off the yoke of Soviet control, embracing innovation and individual strength, and defending its accomplishments as a nation, no matter the costs. By looking at evolution in the ring, we can also chart activism of some of the sport's—and the nation's—leading public figures at times of growth and through moments of crisis.

THE SOVIET STYLE

First, let's examine how the sport arrived in the USSR. Boxing as a sport appeared in what would become the USSR at the end of the 1800s. The originators of the Soviet school consisted of three people: Ernest Lustallo, Arkady Kharlampiev and Borys Denysov, who almost simultaneously began to popularize boxing. It's important to note that they brought boxing from abroad.

Heavyweight champion Vitali Klitschko of Ukraine. Las Vegas, NM. 2004.
Photograph by Roger Williams/UPI/Alamy.

Lustallo was a citizen of France, Kharlampiev learned boxing in the Paris Academy of Fine Arts and Denysov returned from captivity after WWI with a basic knowledge of European boxing. What would become the Soviet school of boxing mimicked the jabbing and footwork that originated in Europe.

While boxing in each of the empire's republics had its own style and emphasis, a more monolithic "Soviet school" took shape. It is built on several characteristics: continuous movement of the feet, constant jabbing—especially direct punches—and fighting at medium and long-distance ranges. These fighters took minimal risks and gleaned maximum benefit. The style also had its limitations: Soviet athletes did not fight well "inside" (a situation in a fight when the athletes' bodies are as close as possible) and had no clinch maneuvers (when one fighter puts another in a hold). The limited ability to fight inside was eventually admitted even by Soviet trainers, though the first manual on close combat came out in the USSR in 1969—well after other athletes around the globe had incorporated the maneuvers into their strategy.

What did it take to be a Soviet fighter? Endurance and physical strength, for starters. Personality and individualism weren't required—those characteristics were discouraged in almost every facet of Soviet life. A cultural goal was the construction of a society where everyone was interchangeable and no one stood out from the crowd. This was true even in boxing, where it became popular both for the stars and also for its ubiquity: every state organization had a boxing group, and coaches developed regimented training, spanning from novice to the top level, wherein every boxer learned the same defensive tactics and attack maneuvers. Despite this uniformity, certain athletes distinguished themselves—i.e., they won more—and were summoned to Moscow, where they represented USSR in local and international competition.

THE UKRAINIAN BOXER: PRECURSORS AND PROTOTYPES

Even as the USSR sold the concept of the ideal Soviet boxer, there were athletes who resisted efforts at standardization. This was almost a miracle, as the whole system of preparation of the novice athlete to elite competitor was planned using exacting standards, and one could only successfully exist in that system by adhering to clear rules. Some early Ukrainian boxers notably broke those rules.

One was Semyon Trestin (1940–1995) from Odesa. The papers called him "the Unbeatable Trestin" because of the mastery of his movements, his ability to absorb opponents' attacks and turn them to his advantage in stealthy counterattacks. He became a star in the featherweight category, with victories in all but 14 of his 262 amateur matches.

After a series of wins, authorities suggested that he represent the capitol of the USSR. Trestin didn't want to leave his beloved Odesa and, after rejecting their invitation, he experienced several strange defeats. Most notable was the USSR championship in 1964, wherein Trestin met Muscovite Stanislav Stepashkin, who was already a European and Olympic champion. The Ukrainian dominated so strongly that the Moscow public went so far as to boo their hometown fighter. However, the judges were tallying scores with a thumb on the scales, and they ruled Stepashkin's performance victorious.

Things kept going poorly for "the Unbeatable Trestin" within the Soviet system. In 1968, Trestin qualified for the Olympics, but a week before he was supposed to leave for Mexico, another athlete was selected for his spot. No explanation or reason was provided, but later, the sports committee hinted to the Ukrainian that he should have been on the "right" side if he'd wanted a better outcome. Basically, he'd been punished for refusing to box for Moscow.

Oleksandr Yahubkin (1961–2013) was another Ukrainian boxer who faced oppression within the Soviet system. As a 19-year-old heavyweight, he was already defeating experienced opponents in the adult category with his strong punch. "Yahubkin was like a fly," said Vasyl Bruchko, a former Soviet boxing champion. "You couldn't say that he was a heavyweight by looking at him. He was simply a gift from god. He had incredible speed, tactics. He had his moves, like in chess."

Yahubkin was considered a top candidate in the 1980 Olympics, but the team leaders gave the place to the Russian Petr Zaev. They argued that the young Ukrainian would later have a chance. But that chance never came; in 1984, the USSR boycotted the tournament, which was being held in the US. Yahubkin's professional career was similarly stymied by the authorities in Moscow. After participating in an unapproved fight in Ecuador against Luis Castillo, state leadership blocked his travel for his next international opportunity: against Mike Tyson, in Japan, for the world championship. Yahubkin never would go pro.

Trestin and Yahubkin were the most vivid examples of Ukrainian boxers who suffered during the Soviet rule, but there were many more. Despite the propaganda aimed at these men and careers that were stymied, they were and remain the pride of their hometowns. Stories and legends about them are passed on from generation to generation. People are proud that they live on the same street that Yahubkin had lived on, and Odesa has hosted a tournament Trestin's memory for 24 years.

THE 1990S: NEW NATION, NEW STARS

The vote for independence in 1991 was a ticket to freedom not only for the peoples of the former USSR, but also for

Ukrainian boxing. Newly liberated from the yoke of Soviet propaganda and the notion that the peoples of the Union could not achieve anything significant without Moscow, Ukrainian fighters proved they could do even better in independence. Ukrainian boxers quickly identified their individual strengths and began to develop them in a way that had not been permitted in the Soviet system.

The development was important for audiences, too. While politicians were building international relations, athletes took up the same project by competing on the international stage. It was a meaningful introduction to Ukraine for worldwide audiences, and for fans in the new nation, boxing was more than entertainment; it was an expression of their identity, one independent of Russia.

Case in point: after several Ukrainian fighters were prevented from participating in the Olympics over the years, the 1990s were transformational. In the 1992 Olympics, a team of united republics of the former USSR participated. A Ukrainian won a boxing prize for the first time since 1980; Rostyslav Zaulychniy went home with a silver medal. Ukraine didn't need Moscow to assert its expertise.

Things went even better in 1996. In Ukraine's first Summer Olympics appearance under its own flag, Volodymyr Klitschko brought home Ukraine's first gold. Volodymyr's style of fighting—a hurricane of punches from all sides, minimum risk and maximum benefit—carried some similarities to the Soviet school of boxing from which he emerged. But Volodymyr worked aggressively, was versatile and attacked from different angles. He switched coaches and became a more pragmatic, dynamic fighter with time. His huge stature, even among heavyweights—6' 6"—also helped him in the ring.

His brother, Vitaly Klitschko, was no less of a unique athlete—and, at 6' 7", no less of a physical presence. Vitaly had hardly spent any time absorbing the Soviet style of boxing—he was too busy as a kickboxer, for which he was a six-time world champion. To convert to boxing, his coach utilized his individual strength and expertise, rather than what was written in the manuals. He entered the ring with a non-standard stance and a lowered front hand; he had lots of movement on defense and was often aiming for a knockout punch. In short: as a fighter, he threw away the old Soviet manual—and in that way, he might be considered the first real representative of Ukrainian professional boxing. He was the first—but not the last—Ukrainian champion to build a style out of his individual strengths.

The simultaneous debut of the Klitschko brothers as professionals, also in 1996, was a breakthrough and provided an entrance for Ukrainian boxers into a field that had been closed off before. It was through these brothers' professional boxing careers, even more than the stellar Olympic performance, that the world learned about Ukraine. The brothers were clearly powerful, absolutely unusual and completely separate from Russian boxing. Both brothers quickly rose to prominence—Volodymyr became the first Ukrainian to fight professionally in the US, with a technical knockout in the sixth round against Carlos Monroe in his debut, and Vitaly became the world champion in 1999.

It's notable that, as the Klitschkos were establishing Ukraine as a powerhouse of professional boxing, Soviet boxing was unable to make the leap into the professional ring. The kind of boxing taught in the USSR was not adaptable to contemporary professional boxing, and the style became non-competitive, perishing along with the state. Further, the stereotype of Drago-style fighting followed many fighters from the former USSR, and promoters were slow to sign professional contracts with them, believing them to be boring and monotonous boxers.

2000S: NEW LEADERSHIP, ESTABLISHED DOMINANCE

The start of the 2000s was an important stage in the careers of both Klitschko brothers and in the evolution of a modern Ukraine. Vitaly's heated battle against Lennox Lewis in 2003—one of the best in the history of heavyweight matches—made him a worldwide celebrity. That meant the spotlight was on him in 2004, when the Orange Revolution started on November 22, 2004. Ukrainians gathered on the Maidan (the main square in Kyiv) to protest the preliminary results of the presidential election, which seemed to suggest that Victor Yanukovych had won over Viktor Yushchenko. They claimed the election was rigged in Yanukovych's favor. Before the election, Russian protégé Victor Yanukovych had solicited Vitaly's support, though the boxer did not endorse him; he and his brother were in Yushchenko's corner.

Vitaly remembers those fraught days after the election: "I was preparing for a fight when I found out that people came

> **BOXING WAS ... AN EXPRESSION OF THEIR IDENTITY, ONE THAT WAS INDEPENDENT FROM RUSSIA.**

WITCHES OF INSTAGRAM #HEXPUTIN

On March 31, 2022, Ukrainian witches gathered near Kyiv to curse Vladimir Putin with "isolation, ousting from power and loss of support from the inner circle."

Witches around the world have also participated in an ongoing hex of Putin, started by American author Michael M. Hughes.

SELECTED ELEMENTS OF THE RITUAL:

Gather blue and yellow candles, sunflower seeds, photo of Putin and sigil.

LIGHT CANDLES.

Call on the "Angels of the Heavens and demons of the underworld" to bring ruin on Putin and bless Ukraine.

Drop the sunflower seeds onto Putin.

Burn the picture of Putin while chanting "гори" (pronounced "Guh-REE," meaning "Burn!").

LAUGH OUT LOUD AT THE ASHES OF PUTIN.

---

out onto the Maidan. I even wanted to cancel the fight and return to Kyiv. But the trainer refused to let me, and we used the ring as a tribute." What happened in the ring made his point: On December 11, Klitschko won against Danny Williams in Vegas through a technical knockout in the eighth round. Vitaly wore an orange ribbon on his shorts in support of the protest. After the fight, he announced, "I support the fight of the people for democracy and against manipulation. For me, the future of my people is very important, and I'll do everything I can."

A few days later, the Klitschko brothers were back in Ukraine and on the Maidan, supporting the protests. The result of the peaceful protests was another round of presidential elections, in which Victor Yushchenko won. Ukrainians were watching Vitaly take this more outspoken political role, but society wasn't quite ready for an athlete-politician. Vitaly's first mayoral campaign, in 2006, didn't succeed, though he continued to play a part in Ukrainian politics, serving on the city council and later in the national parliament.

In 2008, Vitaly returned to the ring. It was, without exaggeration, a spectacle. After the four-year break, he met right away with the champion of knockouts, Sam Peter. Klitschko masterfully boxed against the powerful Peter, who had only lost only once before—to Volodymyr Klitschko. With that victory, the Klitschkos became the first brothers in the history of heavyweights to hold titles at the same time. They continued to dominate the sport for an extremely long time and were perceived by the world boxing community as epoch-making figures, towering for more than just their stature.

Concurrent with their work in the ring, the brothers were working around it. They started K2 Promotions, in order to promote Ukrainian athletes to audiences abroad. Since 2002, there had been two promotional companies in Ukraine—Union Boxing and National Box Promotion—but neither had the clout to fill the large halls and sign contracts with big-name athletes. The brothers' names made it possible to get larger venues, like the Palace of Sports in Kyiv for 10,000 viewers, as well as sign contracts with popular athletes. In 2009, for the first time in the history of Ukraine, a match for the world championship title took place on Ukrainian soil. Ukrainians Viacheslav Senchenko and Yuriy Nuzhnenko battled it out in Donetsk.

Meanwhile, Ukrainian dominance in the amateur sport was not done. In 2008, in Beijing, Ukraine won its second Olympic championship. Vasyl Lomachenko outboxed five opponents with a total score of 58-13 and became the first Ukrainian to receive the Val Barker Trophy, the prize for the best technical score of the tournament.

What was driving this new dominance? The success of Ukrainian amateur boxing can be seen in its approach to training. Anatoliy Lomachenko, Vasyl's father, was one of the founding drivers of this new approach. He emphasized passionate, functional training and masterful work on mid-distance fighting. Under Anatoliy's guidance, Ukrainians boxers looked nothing like the Soviet boxers of the previous generation: they were fast, flexible and versatile athletes. This new style was on magnificent display in 2012, as Ukrainian boxers dominated another Olympic competition with two gold, one silver and two bronze medals.

No less important was the cultural breakthrough that the team achieved in the world boxing community. Lomachenko gave Ukrainian flags as gifts to his competitors before each match. (Notoriously, in 2008, Russian fighter Albert Selimov would not accept the flag before their Olympic meeting; Lomachenko subsequently beat him 14-7.) Oleksandr Usyk and the 2012 silver medalist Denis Berinchyk entered the ring with Cossack hair styles. After their victories, the boxers danced the *hopak*, a Ukrainian folk dance.

These gestures were appreciated by fans. Ukrainian society, which was living under the leadership of Russia protégé Yanukovych (who was elected in 2010), needed a dose of Ukrainian pride. They got it in the boxing ring, a place they loved with their whole hearts.

2010S: THE EUROMAIDAN REVOLUTION

The Maidan started as a peaceful protest at the end of November 2013, in response to an unexpected change in the course of the country's development. Ukraine was on its way to signing a treaty with the European Union when then-president Viktor Yanukovych announced that Ukraine would sign a treaty with the Eurasian Economic Union—in other words, Russia—instead. Protesters were wary of returning to Russian influence—it had spread narratives of dominance for decades, and many worried the country had the goal of conquering Ukrainian lands and destroying Ukrainian cultural identity once again.

Vitaly Klitschko had already expressed how important he felt it was that Ukraine turn toward Europe, and he was building a coalition around it. In 2012, he said, "I never dreamed of being a politician, but today, I took on the responsibility of building a team. We are looking for people who see that Ukraine is a European state. We enter politics not for money, fame, mandates, not for inviolability." So it came as no surprise that he established himself as one of the head figures of the revolution, calling for self-identification and absolute separation from Russia. These peaceful protests turned violent, and more than 100 people were killed in Yanukovych's attempts to forcefully suppress the demonstrations.

Eventually, Yanukovych fled from prosecution to his patron Putin in Russia, and Vitaly Klitschko was one of the main candidates for the presidency in Ukraine. Although he dropped out of the presidential elections—there was some question about whether he qualified for the role, given the years he had lived abroad—the citizens of Ukraine were ready to embrace Klitschko as a political leader. After decades of showing Ukrainians his athletic accomplishments in the ring, in the Euromaidan revolution he demonstrated his civic leadership in the public square. On May 25, 2014, Vitaly Klitschko became the mayor of Kyiv.

> YOU COULDN'T SAY THAT HE WAS A HEAVYWEIGHT BY LOOKING AT HIM. HE WAS SIMPLY A GIFT FROM GOD.

Of being an elected leader, Klitschko said, "Being the mayor of the capital is much harder than being a world champion. I boxed two to three times a year, and now every day is like a fight, and it's not easy. In the ring, you have one opponent, but as mayor, there are many challenges, and you must respond immediately. If before I was watched by spectators in the arena who watched the fight, now they watch me every day. You have no right to make a mistake, and you must bring a winning result." While running the capital city of Ukraine has its own particular ledger of successes and losses, the people of the city have been happy with his scorecard: he has been reelected twice.

2022: WAR AND DEFENSE

On February 24, 2022 the Russian Federation started a full scale invasion into Ukrainian territory. Society needed support and looked for it among its most vivid representatives, which included some of the country's sports heroes. Culturally and ideologically, a Ukrainian boxer is more than an athlete—he is a leader.

The Klitschko brothers were the first to come to defend the country. Volodymyr moved to the capital just a few weeks before the invasion. He signed up for the local defense force responsible for the defense of cities.

From the start, the brothers were in the crosshairs of the Russian troops. Both were singled out as strategic targets. But neither Vitaly nor Volodymyr left Ukraine and its capital. Instead, they expanded their activism, visiting people who were living in the subway during the shelling and visiting soldiers. While Vitaly focused on political and organizational projects, Volodymyr proceeded with social campaigns. The brothers had founded the Klitschko Foundation, and Volodymyr was associated with dozens of charities in Europe, as well as universities abroad. He used all of these connections for the benefit of Ukraine. As his brother Vitaly said during the first weeks of the conflict, "It's difficult to evaluate the level of humanitarian aid which Volodymyr is organizing. There are tons of goods for the suffering and full trucks from his partners."

The Klitschko brothers weren't the only boxers to step in to support the Ukrainian cause. From the first days of the war, Oleksandr Usyk was helping Ukrainians. He started the charitable Usyk Foundation, supported soldiers and visited the wounded. In one of those meetings, the military persuaded him to go for a rematch against Anthony Joshua and help Ukrainians by doing what he does best. The war sharpens basic human needs, and one of those was to instill a dose of national pride. Usyk could get revenge against the British champion and help Ukraine by using his international platform to share information about the conflict.

Well before the fight, Usyk got to work with information dissemination. He exposed Russian falsehoods, reporting the truth—that Russia invaded Ukraine and is bombing peaceful cities (rather than military facilities, as they claimed). As the match approached, Usyk personally negotiated a free broadcast for Ukrainians: Usyk proposed to the promoters that he'd pay for the fight to be broadcast in Ukraine. The promoters decided to show it in Ukraine for free. Moreover, Usyk brought 10 Ukrainian soldiers to the fight in Jeddah—the ones who had persuaded him to agree to the fight—with his own money.

For the press conference before the fight—dubbed the "Rage on the Red Sea"—Usyk reverted back to the Cossack hair style he'd worn at the Olympics. He came to the match in traditional Ukrainian dress and then on stage sang "Oi u luzi chervona kalyna," which had been performed by the archers of the Sich Riflemen (a Ukrainian military group in WWI). In 2022, this song was adopted as an anthem for the Ukrainians in their fight against the Russian invasion. The August 2022 12-round battle—which Usyk won in a split decision—was watched by a record number of Ukrainians. (The official broadcast was watched by more than one million viewers, but the fight was shown on other publicly accessible television stations, so the total number of viewers is likely several times higher.)

The fight was the latest example of how boxing fandom has been tied to Ukrainian identity—a lineage that stretches back through several rounds of Olympic success and into the years when Ukrainian boxers were punished for pushing against the forces of Moscow but found Ukrainian supporters anyway. For decades, the USSR wanted to make everything Ukrainian Soviet; during this invasion, Ukrainians feel the same forces being asserted by the Russian government. So, if a Ukrainian boxer as talented as Usyk announces his Ukrainian position, fans will support him through the final punch.

THE NEXT GENERATION OF FIGHTERS

The new generation of Ukrainian boxers is a direct reflection of the nation's independence. Their fighting has evolved, even as compared to current stars Lomachenko and Usyk. The younger athletes, who haven't lived in the USSR a single day, are absolutely free of the dogma that was systematically drilled into the heads of previous generations. Ukrainian coaches are no longer tied to rote manuals of an earlier era; instead, they teach versatile and exciting boxing.

Who are Ukrainians looking toward as the next generation of boxing talent? Among the top stars of the amateur ring are Oleksandr Khyzhniak and Yuriy Zakharieiev. Khyzhniak is an aggressive puncher who works on attacking the entire match and literally breaks opponents due to his physical endurance. Zakharieiev is of a different mold: he is smart technically and can punch from all corners, switching easily between the first punch and counterpunch.

The professional circuit also shows promise. Karen Chukhadzhian is a talented young fighter. Technical and flexible, he is both difficult to catch with a punch or trap on the ropes. At the same time, Chukhadzhian masterfully manipulates opponents and is known to end fights early with his knockouts. Super heavyweight Vladyslav Sirenko is crafty at knockouts, and can cut corners well. He, like the athletes a generation before him, understands his role as a Ukrainian athlete, especially in a time of crisis: "In my opinion, every athlete who plays under the Ukrainian flag should have a clear political position," he said. "Supporting Ukraine is something that every Ukrainian should do, no matter what their sphere of activity. After our victory, boxing will grow faster, become more inspiring. Like our whole country. When the time is right, there will be plenty of tournaments. The Ukrainian athlete is now a symbol of the struggle."

Sirenko is just one boxer, but he is speaking for the whole sporting community. Boxers and coaches who have never felt Soviet oppression were able to accomplish something that wasn't possible during the USSR, and they are now being pushed to employ that new expertise and leadership in the current war. But this is just the beginning. Ukrainian boxing is now versatile, vivid and strong. Like Ukraine itself. ✻

ZONE OF ALIENATION

Date of Chernobyl nuclear explosion: **APRIL 26, 1986**	Number of people evacuated: **200,000**	**AMOUNT OF RADIATION RELEASED:** at least 50 to 185 million curies of radionuclides (many times the radiation of Hiroshima and Nagasaki combined).
Distance from Kyiv: 65 miles		

Inside the 1,600 square mile Chernobyl Nuclear Power Plant Zone of Alienation, you can find:

1 ABANDONED AMUSEMENT PARK

7,000 WORKERS on rotating shifts to continually monitor and decommission the reactor.

SOME 100,000 TOURISTS A YEAR
who take legal tours. At the entrance, hawkers sell T-shirts, key rings & glow-in-the-dark "Chernobyl condoms," branded with radiation signs.

ILLEGAL TRESPASSERS INSPIRED BY THE VIDEO GAME S.T.A.L.K.E.R., WHO SNEAK IN CARRYING ONLY FOOD, WATER & CHEAP RADIATION METERS. EVERY 3 DAYS, A "STALKER" IS CAUGHT, FINED & DRIVEN TO A POLICE STATION IN IVANKIV.

2 ABANDONED CITIES:
Chernobyl & Pripyat

187 abandoned villages & small communities

1 PRIEST who ministers to workers & Babushkas at the Church of Saint Elias.

1 NEW BABY:
MARIYKA SOVENKO (B. 1999) IS THE ONLY CHILD BORN IN THE ZONE POST-DISASTER. SHE LIVED THERE FULL-TIME UNTIL SHE WAS 7 AND LEFT TO ATTEND SCHOOL. HER BIRTH WAS INITIALLY COVERED UP BY UKRAINIAN AUTHORITIES.

AROUND 200 "SELF-SETTLERS,"
mostly women in their 70s and 80s, who illegally returned. The women, nicknamed "Babushkas of Chernobyl," snuck back to their villages, where they tend their gardens, drink water from their wells and pay each other social calls.

CANNED RADIOACTIVE VEGETABLES, DRIED MUSHROOMS & HOMEMADE SPIRITS, CONSUMED BY THOSE LIVING IN THE ZONE.

300-900 WILD DOGS,
descendants of pets who avoided being shot by liquidators after the explosion.

Boar, elk, roe deer, lynx, bison, wolves & herds of Przewalski's horse. The Zone constitutes the 3rd-largest nature reserve in mainland Europe.

Iconic Ukraine
Alight's Aid2Art program

AS THE WAR IN UKRAINE SPREAD in March of 2022, citizens in Lviv began removing paintings from museum walls and covering statues in protective material in an effort to protect historic works of art. Around the same time, an open-source list of Ukraine-based creatives circulated among global artist networks to connect people to work opportunities. Upon learning about these two very different efforts to support and preserve the artistic work, Alight, an international humanitarian organization working with those displaced by the war, decided to create a new program that would support the basic needs of Ukrainian artists and designers, while providing space for creative expression. "A life is filled with joy, dignity, connection and purpose," the organization states in its mission. "And that's what we aim to build."

Titled Aid2Art, the program provided hundreds of unconditional cash transfers of $1,000 to Ukrainian creatives, giving a lifeline to families who had lost substantial income due to the war. Artists were also invited to submit works on the theme "Iconic Ukraine." The works, including photography, paintings and graphic design, soon became part of a virtual gallery showcasing a wide variety of interpretations of the theme: A firefighter tackles a raging inferno; a curtain catches a gust of wind through a window; a little girl shelters behind wooden shutters; a person looks to the sky as if hopeful for a future without war.

The online gallery, Aid2Art.org, is open to all, and sales of the works benefit Ukrainian artists. One contributing artist said her piece was inspired by a lyric from a popular song by the Ukrainian band Kazka: "She cried and the violet blossomed again..." The song reminded her of her past life before the war; then, she would imagine women crying for various reasons. "Now, we cry more than before," she says. "We are often ashamed of our tears or hold it back. Sometimes, we manage to break free, sing and cry, and it helps."

"Each piece of work came with a powerful description bringing it to life," said Shamaila Usmani, Creative Connector at Alight. "Beauty and creative expression are such a big part of our work. We see beauty and creativity as ways to bring humanity together. Just because someone is going through an unprecedented tough time doesn't mean these things aren't of value to them." ✻

Gaidamaka, "Tree of Life."

Vladyslav Musiienko, "Kyiv."

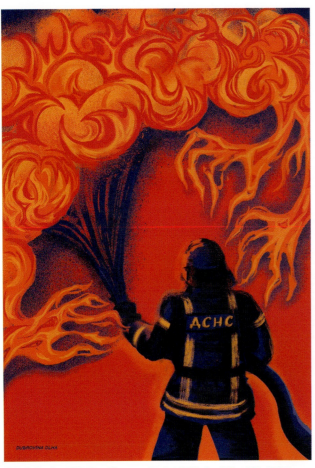
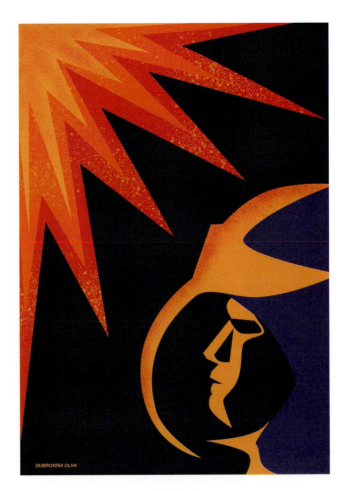

Olha Dubrovina, "The State Emergency Service Of Ukraine | Day 150, 151."

Anastasiia Lytvyn, "In a Bright Future." 2022.

Masha Raymers, "Ukrainian Soul." 2022.

Natalia Azarkina, from the series "Between Darkness and Light."

Olena Chekhovska, *"Shelter."*

Yaroslav Boruta, *"Flower of Despair."* 2022.

Dmytro Kupriyan, *"Home."* 2020.

Ruslana Maistruk, "Tree of Life of Ukraine." 2022.

Ruslana Maistruk, "War Series: Don't be afraid. I'm with you." 2022.

Mariia Lytovchenko, "Chumaks Way."

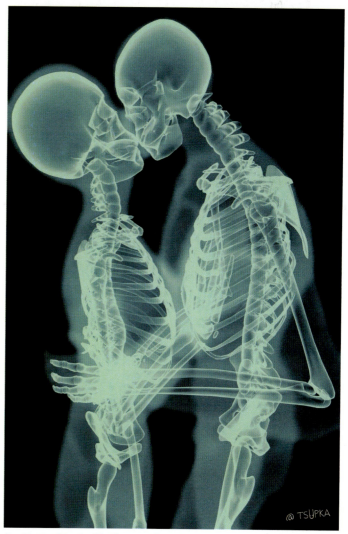

Ivan Tsupka, "Kiss from Xray" amateur photo series.

FICTION

Knock Knock
Lily Hyde

To knock, стучать: to inform on someone (Russian slang)

"Has someone been knocking again?"

Alim looked at the papers on the desk in front of him. "We've had some information."

"From Baba Katya."

"From a citizen. I can't tell you that."

"Alright, alright." Enver leaned back, trying to sprawl comfortably in the uncomfortable wooden chair. "Go on then. Out with it. What have I done this time?"

"On Tuesday evening this week, you were talking in your kitchen. In Crimean Tatar. About Putin and Islamic State."

Tuesday. Yes, Lenura's parents had been 'round, and they had indeed been speaking Crimean Tatar in the kitchen, over *kobete* hot from the oven and a little bit of *Bitay* Katibe's cherry brandy.

Enver waited for Alim to look up and meet his eye. "Baba Katya doesn't speak Crimean Tatar."

"...No."

"So she can't possibly know, the old dear, that what we were saying about Islamic State was that the idiots who join it need their heads examined, and that Putin, on the other hand, is our adored hero and the sun shines out of his arse."

Alim looked back down at the papers. "I think she does know the Crimean Tatar word for 'arse,' actually."

Enver lowered the front chair legs carefully back to the ground. "How so?"

"Because she also complains that you were talking about your cat. Which likes to shit all over her garden."

Enver snorted so abruptly that a bit of snot flew out of his nose. Alim's lips were twitching, the dimple showing in his cheek.

"Kiss my arse," said Enver in Crimean Tatar, which sounded in Russian a bit like "clever cat." Alim let out a smothered yelp. "Alright, what do I sign? Do I sign something? Or I can publicly flagellate myself down the village high street? Will that do?"

...

He walked out of the police station entrance whistling. There were snowdrops growing by the path outside, clean little scraps of spring. Enver waited for a bit, looking at them vaguely. Then he stepped over and made his way round the building to the back door.

Alim was there smoking a cigarette.

Enver lit up. "So what other misdemeanors of the good citizens of Kamenka have you got from your knocking shop?" he asked, with a good-natured leer. "Who's knocking up whom, for example..." Alim didn't smile this time. "Oh come on, you can tell me. Or am I really the only one anyone ever informs on? I'm flattered."

Photograph by Elena Subach.

"You should really be careful, Enver," Alim said.

"The cat's grounded," Enver promised solemnly. "Don't worry so much! It's not your fault. It's not Baba Katya's fault really. How much does she get each time—2,000 rubles? If they paid her a better pension, she wouldn't do it. Well, actually, she would. She enjoys it, the dear sweet vicious nosy old so-and-so."

"What happened? I remember you used to be great neighbors."

"What happened?" They had been great neighbors once, Enver's two girls forever running 'round for Baba Katya to spoil them rotten with sweets and homemade jam. "Russia happened. And she went completely batshit crazy." Enver winked. "Catshit crazy. On the other hand, you should see Nikita on the other side. My neighboring alcoholic. He's discovered some long-lost family in Siberia, tidied up the yard, donated his spectacular collection of empty vodka bottles to some museum of Russian eternal victory. Now he's forever out there, puttering about and planting and watering things. He's even found money to fix the fence. Hey—" Enver looked at Alim with a sudden idea. "He's not knocking as well, is he? Is that where the money's from?"

Alim looked surprised. "No. Not to me."

"Oh well. Anyway, it's an improvement, I can tell you. I almost feel like I should be planting flowers and writing poetry myself, to keep up with the Joneses and the bedtime stories they tell you."

"I hate hearing them," Alim muttered. "I just really can't stand it." He rubbed his eyes with his knuckles, childishly. Ash fell from the cigarette between his fingers, down his blue uniform shirt.

Enver brushed it off for him. "Meryeshka still keeping you awake all night?" The younger man nodded, face still hidden by his hand. "Can't Elmaz take her to her mother's for a bit? You'd be able to work on the house. And it'd be easier for Elmaz to have her mother there."

"Ilmi's living there with his new wife. Anyway, you know what her mum thinks of me."

Enver could have said something reassuring, but on the other hand, the whole village knew that Elmaz's mother's brief honeymoon with her son-in-law around the time of the wedding had long since soured. He said: "Well, that's why I thought she might be happy to have Elmaz and Meryeshka without you, to be honest. So she can do a bit of subverting back to the Dark Side."

He nudged Alim cheerfully. "As if that'd work. Meryeshka's the spitting image of you; stubborn as a mule up to its arse in oats. When you were in nappies, you howled all night like a banshee, too." Alim still looked pitiful. "Alright, why don't you send them round to us, then?" Hell's teeth, where had that come from? Meryeshka was gorgeous—of course she was, she was a baby—and the funny thing was that she really was the spitting image of Alim, with the red circles in her cheeks and the lick of dark hair standing up from her forehead. But she did howl, not actually like one but like a whole coven of furious banshees, out for blood.

"Elmaz doesn't really like—I mean, she's a bit nervous about trusting Meryeshka with other people," Alim muttered.

"Lenura brought up our two pretty well, despite all my attempts to drop them on their heads or give them a solid grounding in Nietzsche before the age of two," Enver said, deciding not to feel offended. "Hasn't Baba Katya told you about that yet? Oh, she will, she will."

"I don't want to know," Alim said. "I hate this. It's shit, this job. You've got no idea how shit it is now."

Enver could have taken offense at that, too. It had been mostly his idea to encourage Alim into a police career; a regular income, maybe promotion and a right smack in the eye for Elmaz' mother always going on about her friends in the Mejlis and how Crimean Tatars should get into positions of authority to protect national rights.

And it had worked: six months after he got the village police position, Alim and Elmaz had been married. Six months after that, Russia had arrived. So yes, to be fair, shit was probably the word. Enver shrugged, unoffended. "So pack it in."

"How?" the word came out almost a shout. "I've got a baby to feed, Enver! There are the payments on the house. What will Elmaz say if I quit?"

Alim rarely shouted. Crying babies, honestly, they were worse than armies of occupiers. "You could get another job," Enver said. "Elmaz's mother would understand if you asked for an extension on the loan. But you wouldn't need to ask," he added, at the look on Alim's face. Mothers-in-law, Hell's teeth, they were worse than crying babies. "There's other work around. I could get you in at the taxi firm, I'll ask Emine."

> WHO WOULD I EVEN BE, IN KYIV? NOBODY. CRIMEA'S MY HOME, AND I'M STAYING. I'D BE A TRAITOR TO ABANDON IT.

"You haven't got enough work there for yourself."

"I started taking less. I told you, I want to cultivate my garden and write poetry, like a disgraced Chinese Imperial official. Or there's building work—all those new cottages down near Koreiz. I'll ask Dilyaver. Handy bastard like you, you can get work."

Alim put his cigarette out slowly and deliberately against the wall. "It's not so bad, really," he said, looking at the stub squashing and squashing against the dirty plaster. "We got new boots; look." He stuck out a black-booted foot, dropped the stub and ground it under the sole. "I told you we got a new boss in Bakhchisaray. He's Dagestani. I get time off for Friday Namaz now."

"But you don't go to Namaz," Enver pointed out. He'd recently started going to the mosque on Fridays himself, but Alim had never shown an interest. "You're not solid and respectable enough." Alim didn't even have a disreputable policeman's beer gut; he was looking positively scrawny these days.

"I've got to get back." Alim turned to go inside.

Enver raised a hand. "Mention it to Elmaz, about coming 'round to us for a night or two. And I'll do something absofucking-tastic for Baba Katya to inform you about next time. It'll be the dog's bollocks, my friend. You'll get a fat bonus, and you can finally quit on the back of it. You better give me a cut, mind."

He walked back through the village, wondering how he was going to persuade Lenura to invite Elmaz and Meryeshka 'round for a couple of nights, while he himself went off somewhere else. He'd take Alim away fishing—that was it—like he had in the old days when Alim was a teenager busy going to the bad side, eyes too big for his skinny face and knees poking out the holes in his jeans, and Enver had decided to take him on because he needed fixing. A couple of days fishing'd get the poor doleful bugger back together.

Back home, Nikita was out on one side, doing something with a hoe. On the other, Baba Katya was putting crumbs on the bird table Enver had helped her put up. Enver had been one of the lucky ones when he'd returned to Crimea 20 years ago; he'd managed to buy an existing house in the village. But as the saying went, you don't buy a house, you buy neighbors. It was a shame, really, because while all Nikita had ever contributed had been a rubbish- and rat-infested yard and the occasional drunken knife fight, Katya had been a great neighbor. She'd been a marvel of comfort and good sense through all the shrieks, sulks, doom and despair that had accompanied Enver's daughters' awful boyfriends or disappointing exam results, while all their father had been able to do was make inappropriately humorous remarks.

Enver leaned over the fence, big with contrition. "Afternoon, Baba Katya. I'd like to apologize for our cat—" he began innocently, but of course his big gob ran away with him "—cat's arse and its predilection for defecating in your garden. And I promise that next time we're discussing Islamic State, we'll do it in Russian and invite you 'round for your valued contribution."

...

"Knock knock?"

"We've had some information." Today, the accumulating papers in front of Alim were in a gray cardboard folder.

"I haven't even done it yet!" Enver complained. "It's still in the early planning stages, and if she's informed on me about it, she's been reading my mind, the old witch."

Alim didn't look up. "You've started going to Friday Namaz."

"I know," Enver said, a bit taken aback. He was sensitive about his attendance at the mosque; it was like a little, new-found tender shoot that had sprouted inside him, inexplicable even to himself. "And you know. *You* get permission from the great Russian state to take time off from policemanly duties to go to Friday Namaz. It's practically a civic regulation, like the boots. Respectable people go to Namaz."

"And you slaughtered a sheep for last Bayram."

"So did half the village. And we gave Baba Katya a big chunk. Not my fault it was chewy as leather."

"You're growing a beard, she says."

"I am *not* growing a beard! Lenura'd leave me for our clean-shaven newly spick-and-spiffing-span neighbor Nikita if I grew a beard. I haven't shaved for a few days because it's spring and I'm allergic to pollen and I get this rash. Not just on my chin. Do you want me to share with Baba Katya all the highly personal details?"

"She's—the citizen's—concerned about your piety."

"My *what?*"

"Your piety," Alim repeated expressionlessly.

"I think Baba Katya might need a dictionary. I mean, the word impious was invented with me in mind...." Alim still wouldn't move his gaze from the folder. "Alright, alright. Hang on a minute. I'll take the oath and do the penance." He waited for Alim to look at him, then held up his hand in a Pioneer salute and recited, piously: "Thou shalt honor Putin and the Russian state; thou shalt not covet thy neighboring state's freedom of speech and religion..."

...

Where the snowdrops had been by the police station entrance was a thick patch of violets now. Their sweet scent vanished in the warm air almost as he noticed it. Enver breathed in slowly. Out. Then, he went 'round to the back.

SPOT THE UKRAINIAN

QUIZ: Which of these famous "Russians" are actually from Ukraine?

NINA PETROVNA KHRUSHCHEVA
As wife of Soviet Premier Nikita Khrushchev, was the first Russian political spouse to act as First Lady.

LEON TROTSKY
Communist theorist and agitator who helped lead Russia's 1917 October Revolution and was exiled.

SERGEI KOROLEV
Regarded as founder of the Soviet space program; rocket engineer during the space race.

NIKOLAY GOGOL
Author of one of the great Russian novels of the nineteenth century, *Dead Souls*.

LEONID ZHABOTINSKY
Soviet weightlifter who won gold medals in the 1964 and 1968 Olympics and set 19 world records.

VERA KHOLODNAYA
The first Russian silent movie star, earning the title "Queen of Russian Cinema."

YAKOV SMIRNOFF
Stand-up comedian best known for "Russian reversal" jokes.

ANSWER KEY: *They are all from Ukraine or have Ukrainian roots.*

"Do you think Baba Katya's seeing some potential conversion in me that I haven't seen yet?" he asked, lighting up next to Alim on the back step. "Maybe I should send you to warn Lenura to hide all the alcohol before I get home. Just turn a blind eye to all the banned Islamic literature lying around, won't you?"

"Enver." Alim had the same harrassed look as when he'd made the pioneer salute inside. "You really shouldn't go 'round saying things like that."

"Yes but I'm saying them to you," Enver pointed out.

"That's—" Alim started a gesture, and then let his hands fall to his sides.

"It's either you or Tolik, and you're more fun." Tolik, dim, torpid and Ukrainian, was the village's other policeman. He'd been on the job forever and was as bent as a dog's back leg, but fortunately too lazy to fully take advantage of his own bentness. "Why is it always you and not him on the knocking desk, anyway?"

"I don't know. Because they know how much I hate it," Alim said. He was already on his second fag. He looked exhausted, worse than last time. "Stop joking about it."

"Have you *seen* my beard? Exactly. Sherlock Holmes'd need a fucking magnifying glass. Has Russia started issuing regulation police magnifying glasses yet, to spot the microscopic signs of extremism?" He cut off whatever Alim was going to say. "Have you asked Elmaz about coming 'round to stay with us?"

Alim shook his head. "Is there any work with the taxi firm?"

"Emine's been busy," Enver replied evasively yet encouragingly. "So you see, yes, probably loads of work."

In fact, he had asked Emine a few days ago if she could take on another driver. Emine had been doubtful; the firm was suffering from the influx of drivers from Donbas pushing down prices. Still, they were here today, gone tomorrow, and the tourist season was coming up—maybe there actually would be a tourist season this year.

"I'll take a few less hours," Enver had said to her. "I want more free time to finish dictating my scandalous memoirs to my neighbor."

"Hmmm?" Emine was scrolling through time sheets on the computer. "He's reliable, I presume. Clean license?"

"He's more than reliable; he's the only clean cop in Crimea. His license is so clean he could wipe his beautiful baby's bottom with it."

Emine's hand stopped twiddling the computer mouse. "A cop—you mean Alim?"

"Yup."

"I don't think so," Emine had said. "Times are hard. No. Sorry."

Enver had been puzzled by the change of tone. "So Alim's a *Chingene** and an orphan who married above himself—is that it? Hardly a sin. And now he's got a family to look after; debts to pay off."

Emine had just said "We've all got family to look after. And Alim will pay for his sins before the Almighty."

No point in repeating that to Alim. "Something'll come up," Enver said now to his friend, whom he'd been looking after like family for years now, because he'd seen something that needed fixing, and he was able to fix anything with a bit of wheeling, a bit of dealing, dealing and dealing the cards until the right one turned, bright side up.

Alim sighed and then cleared his throat, as if hoping Enver wouldn't catch the sad little exhale. "It doesn't matter. I've got to go."

"Me too. Pious deeds are waiting. I've got to carry shopping for helpless old ladies, and recite prayers for the everlastingless of Putin and the Third Fucking Rome."

"Enver."

...

"Knock knock. What's the story this time?"

Alim held the fattening file upright on the desk between them, so not much was visible beyond that lick of dark hair that wouldn't stick down. "You've been using profanity in public."

"Yes...So?" Enver was baffled. "I do, I do use profanity, I admit it, I swear frequently, lavishly, inventively, and sometimes in languages she doesn't understand. Does she quote the exact words?" He tried inquisitively to see round the edge of the folder, but Alim held it firmly. "Baba Katya swears herself. You should hear how she talks about Ukrainians, for example. Shocking."

Alim still didn't say anything. "I don't swear at Baba Katya, by the way. Her dear, sweet, innocent old heart wouldn't take it. Is there a law against swearing these days? Anyway." He rocked forward to lean over the desk. "Any-fucking-way, last time I seem to remember she said—"

"Yes well. That's just it. She says it's 'unbecoming and offensive and suspicious,' coming from such a pious person as yourself."

"...Pardon?"

"A person renowned for his piety. Swearing."

Enver reached out and tugged the folder towards him, so that it fell flat. They stared at each other solemnly across the police desk, waiting to see who would crack.

"Can I laugh?" Enver enquired at last. "Or should you do that first?"

...

Outside the front entrance were daffodils now. Enver watched them bobbing about in the wind before he noticed that Alim's car was parked beyond them. Odd. It was a 15-minute walk from Alim's place to the police station, and Elmaz liked to have the car in the day, to drive Meryeshka around in an attempt get her to sleep.

"Why are you driving to work?" he asked, round at the back door. "Oh, wait, I get it: the boots. How very Russian to carpet Crimea with jackboots, but not bother to check if they fit. Or is it one size fits all? I hate to tell you, but your uniform's too big, too." It was literally hanging off him, now Enver came to look. "Isn't Elmaz feeding you at all these days, Alim? Have you suggested yet that she bring Meryeshka 'round to us for a bit? Lenura'll send her back with her pockets stuffed with *kobete* for you."

"I'm not sure it's a good idea," Alim muttered, 'round the cigarette in his mouth.

"Why not? I may have got a tad more eccentric now my daughters aren't here to keep me in line, but I'm not yet running naked 'round the garden singing the Star-Spangled Banner. Although, come to think of it, Baba Katya—" But Alim wasn't even looking at him waggling his eyebrows suggestively. "You know everything I say; I say it to you," Enver said. "Or if I don't, Baba Katya does."

---

* *Chingene are Crimean Roma. They traditionally played music for weddings and other occasions because Crimean Tatars were forbidden by strict Islam to play music.*

"I don't know what Dilyaver said to you about a building job."

"He didn't say much. Just that he'd talk to his uncle." Enver was a bit disconcerted. In fact, last week, when it became clear that Enver was asking about work for Alim, Dilyaver had said "For that collaborator?"

"Tell him not to bother asking," Alim said. "I don't need your help, Enver. I'm fine where I am. This way, I get to finish the house. I keep my promises, I pay my debts." He gulped the last bit of smoke and threw the stub down, hard. "I've got to go."

It was a bit of luck that on his way home Enver bumped into Sayid coming out of the shop. Sayid was head of a bigger building brigade, with a Russian boss who had work coming out his ears.

But Sayid said straight off: "No."

"Why not? Alim knows his stuff, he's building his own fancy place; it's going to have turrets and everything."

"He's a collaborator," Sayid said flatly, as Dilyaver had said.

"Your wife's a teacher at a state school," Enver pointed out. "We all do what we have to do. Alim—"

"My wife is teaching our children their native language. Your Alim's part of the machine that's repressing us for being Crimean Tatar."

"He's got a kid to feed."

"Islyam Memedov's got two; Ibraim has got four kids to feed, while they're in prison." Sayid leaned close, speaking low and harshly. "Do you really think he doesn't know what you're doing, that stuff you post about what's going on here?"

"That's not me," Enver objected. "I'm just the court jester providing entertainment for that representative of Crimea's god-given rulers, my batty neighbor Katya. Come on, Sayid. You've know Alim since he was bite-sized. There's no harm in him. It's not his fault Russia came along."

"Russia came along three years ago. Why didn't he quit then?"

"So that a policeman as bent as Tolik could've taken his place? Alim's one of us."

"One of us," Sayid repeated. "Have you heard about the Osmanov wedding yesterday, in Kyzyltash?"

"I heard it got raided." Kyzyltash was over the other side of Bakhchisaray, but of course the news had traveled immediately. "Because they were playing Ukrainian folk songs and someone informed on them. I heard they bought themselves off with cake and the musicians' fee and a blast of the Russian national anthem—"

"It was Alim," Sayid said. "Center E, and Tolik and Alim."

"Well, he's *chingene*. He's a bit particular about music." Enver's joke fell flat, even to himself. The musician's fee was all the money the wedding guests held up as they danced in turn with the bride and groom. He'd danced so himself at Alim and Elmaz' wedding. Alim had borrowed hugely and invited everyone; there'd been a long line to dance with beautiful Elmaz like a princess in an embroidered dress that swung like a bell. Alim, hair stubbornly sticking up above his hectic, rosy face, had gleamed and shone opposite Enver. He remembered the feel of the crisp Ukrainian banknotes folded between his fingers.

He said, "If Alim hadn't been there, Tolik would probably have tried to make off with the bride as well."

"One of us," Sayid said again, with total disgust.

"Yes. Sayid, you know how much I appreciate an absurd situation. Everyone's blaming Alim for not quitting his job, but at the same time, no one will give him a job so that he can quit. Something's got to give. He's having a hard enough time trying to be decent and keep up with his debts and responsibilities. Good thing he doesn't realize yet how you're all so prejudiced against him."

"You're a fool, Enver. Why do you think he's started driving to work? So he doesn't have to look any of us in the face on the way. He knows what a traitorous shit he is, even if you don't."

After that conversation, Enver was not in the mood to get a call, as he turned in through his garden gate, from his cousin Ernes in Kyiv. Ernes had left Crimea right after annexation. He called Enver every week or so, urging him to do the same. Enver leaned against the gate, absently watching his neighbor Nikita watering some flowers he'd planted where all the rubbish and old bottles used to be, and tried to listen with his usual tolerance. He appreciated his cousin's concern, especially as it was easy to brush off with jokes. And yet today, he suddenly found himself shouting, to his own surprise, "I'm not going anywhere! Who would I even be, in Kyiv? Nobody. Crimea's my home, and I'm staying. I'd be a traitor to abandon it."

Nikita dropped his watering can and squashed a tulip. Enver gave him an embarrassed wave. "I want to stay and

> **HOW VERY RUSSIAN TO CARPET CRIMEA WITH JACKBOOTS, BUT NOT BOTHER TO CHECK IF THEY FIT.**

cultivate my garden, like whatsisname, Candide," he said into the phone. "I want to plant tulips and daffodils and whatd'youcallits, those frilly pink things."

"...Roses?"

"No, like big pink pompoms. Whatever they're called. Wait, I'll ask Lenura."

"Ask her about leaving," Ernes said. "Promise me you'll talk about it with her, Enver. Now, before they catch up with you. Promise."

"Alright," Enver grumbled. "Leaving, yes, alright. I've got it. I'll think about it." He shoved the phone back in his pocket.

Lenura had gone out for something, leaving a bowl of cake mixture on the kitchen table. Maybe a missing ingredient that, in happier times, she'd have borrowed from Baba Katya. Sighing a bit, Enver scooped out a big glob and ate it, to cheer himself up. He was licking his fingers when someone knocked.

It was Nikita from next door, sober, awkward and clutching two tulips in a plastic bag.

"Afternoon, Enver," he said. "I, er...Sorry, I couldn't help overhearing. Are you really thinking of leaving?"

"I might be," Enver said cautiously. "Why?"

Nikita wordlessly held out the tulips. Enver looked at them. They'd clearly been hastily dug up, grubby bulbs, earwigs and all.

"I know I'm a fantastic neighbor," Enver joked. "But it'll take more than a couple of tulips to persuade me to stay, you know."

Nikita glanced round anxiously. "Actually, that's what I wanted to talk to you about. Can I come in?"

...

Enver only managed to get Alim to come 'round after his shift by promising that Lenura was with Elmaz, and then threatening to come and drag him out of the police station himself, draped in the Ukrainian flag. He installed the policeman at the kitchen table—making sure the window was shut—and laid out Lenura's freshly made cakes, and his own proposal.

"Twenty thousand," Alim said, staring at the lino tablecloth patterned with giant, faded daisies among which unicorns frolicked, chosen long ago by Enver's daughters. "It's not enough."

"A month!" Enver crowed. "What do you mean, it's not enough? Well, of course it's not enough. I'm worth far more than that; I'm priceless. But it's per month, Alim. It'll help cover your debt to your mother-in-law. And once you quit your job, you'll get other work; people'll come 'round. I'll help you out."

"Twenty thousand rubles," Alim murmured again.

"Hey, he offered me 10 to start with, if I stay. I got him up to 20. It's half of what the FSB pays him to watch me. Knock knock! That's who Nikita's long-lost Russian family turned out to be. He told me all about it. No wonder he's turned into such a sober and industrious bloody horticulturalist." The warm cakes in front of the younger man were untouched. Enver reached over and shook the uniform sleeve. "Come on, Alim!"

Alim looked up at last. The habitual high color in his cheeks was sharp and hectic. "Aren't you ever afraid, Enver?"

"Of Nikita? Nikita's so fond of me these days that he's offering me half his FSB blood money if I stay here in Crimea. We're going to plant peonies together and discuss geopolitics and ethics. I'm his cash cow; he's going to make sure I'm in permanent clover. And as it turns out, the FSB is going to pay you to quit your job in the police. Twenty grand! It's perfect. It's fucking genius!"

Alim shook his head. His lips twitched. "Yeah. Yeah, you're a genius, Enver." His gaze slid sideways, to look out of the closed window that faced Baba Katya's house. The cat was sitting on the garden fence, twitching its tail.

"It might be a bit tricky when Baba Katya finds out how much more she could be earning," Enver admitted. "It's a whole new level of keeping up with the Joneses. Well I can always threaten *her* with leaving as well—"

"I think about leaving," Alim said. "I think about taking off for the city, Moscow or Kazan or Istanbul or somewhere. Just me. Some big, anonymous city where no one knows me. I wouldn't take anything; I'd just go. Disappear one night. I can just start all over again."

Enver frowned at him. "You can't do that."

"I know."

"Elmaz, and the baby. The house."

"I know."

"And the cornerstones aren't really rubies and the streets aren't really paved with gold, you know," Enver joked. Alim was smiling, but it was such a bleak smile and his eyes were so darkened that Enver managed to close his big gob on any other frivolous remarks. And yet he just couldn't do despair. It wouldn't fit inside him. That unyielding density would always balloon and squeak and turn up its bright side. He watched in helpless bafflement as Alim rubbed his knuckles into his eyes. The shoulders in their blue uniform shook. But when Alim took his hands away his eyes were dry.

"Sometimes I feel like I'm on a bridge. A very narrow bridge, just one plank wide, and I'm trying so hard to keep my balance. And way down below me, there's the city. All laid out like this—" he held out his hand, the flattened palm upturned towards Enver— "all the streets and houses. Anyone can see everything. All of us down there, running about. Like ants."

For once, not a single joke came to Enver. Outside, the cat dropped down from the fence. A breath later it appeared silently on the windowsill. Its luminous topaz eyes stared at them through the glass, unblinking.

Enver tipped his chair back and reached for the cupboard under the sink. "It's your day off tomorrow, isn't it? Good. What you need, my friend," plonking a bottle of *Bitay* Katibe's cherry brandy on the table between them, "is a drink."

He sent Alim home after less than an hour, when Lenura called to say she was on her way back. They must have met on the way; when Lenura came in, she was disapproving. "Have you two been drinking?" she demanded. "You know he doesn't drink these days. Elmaz doesn't like it."

"It was just a bit." Enver held up the bottle, with a good quarter still glowing ruby-red to prove it. "Believe me, he needed it." So had Enver, if truth be told. "And it worked. He came 'round. He'll be fine. It's fixed. It's all going to be fine."

"So long as he doesn't carry on drinking at home, that's all."

"He won't. What did Elmaz say? Did you persuade her?"

"The poor girl's really lonely, stuck on her own all day." Lenura sat down where Alim had been. "She's coming with Meryeshka on Friday and staying 'til Sunday. Those are Alim's next days off."

Enver looked at his wife with melting, doggy eyes. He tried to infuse into them the sense of a gently wagging tail.

"She's coming early. Five. So you two can go off fishing."

"Lenurochka. You're the queen of my heart."

She threw a cake at him. "Your black, little, scheming, slithering-out heart."

⋯

At five, he shot up in bed, woken by an awful commotion outside the front of the house. Dawn light seeped in through the curtains. Vehicle engines cut out. Doors slammed. Noisy, determined activity. The gate clanged open, clashed shut.

And this was it. They had come for him, just like Ernes said. Like Sayid said, his parents, everyone's parents and grandparents. They had caught him up. It was happening. It was in his blood, his collective memory, yet Enver had never really believed it was possible to happen, he discovered. Not to him. Not this hammering on the front door. Not this brutal dawn assault on his peaceful, sleepy family home, his fortress, everything he had gathered close and safe around him.

Beside him, Lenura stirred and blinked groggy, frightened eyes. Should he kiss her? A few noble parting words? Don't be so melodramatic, Enver. Get dressed? He didn't want to be arrested in his underpants. On the other hand, he didn't want them to kick in the door while he fiddled with buttons and buckles.

"I'll just be a minute——" he said to Lenura, compromising by pulling on tracksuit bottoms while hopping out of the bedroom. Thunderous knock-knock-knocking now from the front of the house. He'd replaced the door just last year; it was nice and new and painted purple. Stumbling through the living room, he realized he hadn't grabbed his phone, hadn't deleted anything, hadn't sent the message that was always there at hand, waiting to be sent, for when this happened. Fat lot of good you are in a crisis, Enver. He opened the front door. Oh Lord, Almighty, I am in Your hands.

Outside on the step were not armed soldiers, not the FSB and Center E in balaclavas and riot gear. Elmaz stood there, holding a hiccuping baby.

Enver's heart came back from wherever it had been off having an attack, and took up residence somewhere around his knees. They trembled. Five a.m.—five a.m., he thought, aghast. Elmaz had gotten the wrong bloody day to come 'round with Meryeshka. He couldn't go fishing now. He hadn't borrowed the fishing rods. He was a bit hungover. He was working from two 'til 10. And then he'd have to come home to someone else's adorable child howling all night.

He said, "Elmaz, love, it was supposed to be next week, Alim's *next* day off, not this one."

Meryeshka wailed. Her black tuft of hair stood straight up; her mouth was a great round "o" between her wet, red, round cheeks. Elmaz' arms held the baby tightly. And then Elmaz opened her mouth, an identical o, the spitting image of desolation and woe.

"What the—Were you really looking forward to it that much?" Enver found himself asking.

Lenura appeared, plump and furry and sleepily cross in her toweling dressing gown. "Or else Alim did keep on drinking and they had a blazing row. Go on, go and see." With one hand, she pushed him out the door while, with the other, she gathered in the wailing mother and child, into the safe warm house.

After a moment, she opened the door again and threw out his jacket and sandals.

Baba Katya's curtains on one side twitched. On the other side, Nikita's door opened; he put 'round it a long nose and a hand holding a watering can. Enver waved and beamed reassuringly. Alim's car was parked outside the gate; he felt like patting it. He set off on still-wobbly knees through the dawn, the beautifully empty, ordinary, miraculous, cool pink dawn, for Alim's place.

Once, it had been just an open-raftered, dirt-floored house with one window and one door, where Alim had lived with his grandmother. That house was still there, like a sort of miniature child's drawing of a home now attached to the new, two-story, fancy building. This was half finished, of course, like all Crimean Tatar houses. The early morning light outlined with meticulous clarity Meryem's toys lying around on the path and steps among buckets and bricks and stacked planks. The front door was unlocked when Enver tried it.

GOT WHEAT?

Ukraine is known as the "bread basket of Europe."

Average Ukrainians eat **190–242 LBS** of bread per year.

(Americans average 53 lbs)

Ukrainian superstition says never to throw away bread—not even crumbs.

The yellow of Ukraine's flag represents its golden wheat fields.

PALYANITSYA is a Ukrainian hearth-baked bread with a distinctive "smiling mouth"—a semi-circular, lateral incision in the bottom third of the loaf.

Russians and Ukrainians pronounce the word palyanitsya (паляниця) *differently. It is reportedly being used as a shibboleth to uncover Russian saboteurs by asking them to say the word and prove if they are friend or foe.*

WHEAT CHIPS DOMINATE OVER POTATO CHIPS ON UKRAINIAN MARKET SHELVES

Korovai, an intricately decorated sweet bread served at weddings, can only be made by a happily married woman and can only be placed in the oven by a happily married man. The bakers are said to pass the fate of their own marriage to the new couple. It is considered a bad omen if the korovai cracks while baking.

POPULAR PATRIOTIC TATTOOS INCLUDE:

The word паляниця *(bread)*

Images of bread

Wheat stalks

"Alim?" He shouted. "Alim! Alim! Alim!"

No one answered. Silence flowed from the house, past him into the spring morning and dissolved in a silver rinsing of birdsong. Enver had the sudden, incontrovertible sense that there was no one in the house to answer.

"Oh my giddy aunt," he said, aloud. "He's done it. He's actually taken off; he's gone to Moscow or Kazan, like he said." The words fell into stillness. "Alim! Alim!"

He ran up the stairs; opened doors onto empty rooms; slowly came down again. The low sun slanted into the big kitchen and living space, turning the bare walls pink, the floating dust motes to soundless specks of light. Soon, Enver thought he would feel angry, disappointed, bereft. Betrayed. But right now, he was suspended in a pure and limpid amazement, tinged with a tiny, rosy flush of admiration. "You left. Alim, you little—"

When had he gone? How? He hadn't taken the car; Elmaz had driven it up to their house. Had he just wandered away alone like the nomad he was, into the morning with a *lyepushka* and an apple from the winter store, wrapped in a spotted handkerchief over his shoulder?

Enver opened the door to the storeroom, that had once been the poor, mean, single-roomed house where Alim had grown up with his grandmother.

He nearly bashed his face against the dangling knees. The pair of feet, in regulation black police boots, tapped gently and insistently on his chest. Knock, knock.

The world made one violent lurch and swung. He was standing, balanced, on the narrow, soiled plank of the threshold, and far below him lay the city, with all its streets and houses, its towers and domes and minarets. From above where the boots hung, the city shone like a ruby, like a single, precious carved jewel suspended far below in the darkness. ❋

What Began in Maidan Continues
Voices from the Revolution of Dignity

Kristina Berdynskykh

THE YEAR WAS 2004, and protests were sweeping through Kyiv. I was in my 20s, supporting the demonstrations as a university student, and I remember feeling a rush of pride in my country. Maybe, I realized, ordinary Ukrainian citizens like me had the power to finally change our society.

I was born in Kherson, in the south of Ukraine. At the time, the Soviet Union still existed. In 1990, I attended a Soviet school. Only a year later, after the USSR collapsed, I was in an independent Ukrainian school. My family and I lived poorly, and my parents divorced when I was 10. Ever since I can remember, I have wanted to escape from my depressing hometown.

Luckily, I was accepted into a university in Mykolaiv, also in the south. It was a time of promise: as a result of the 2004 protests in Kyiv's Independence Square, our Maidan Nezalezhnosti, we managed to achieve peaceful and fair elections. The pro-Ukrainian—not pro-Russian—candidate won.

Unfortunately, after the victory of the 2004 revolution, not much changed in Ukraine. Corruption did not disappear, oligarchs remained powerful and the economy did not improve. Despite this, people still had a sense of what freedom and democracy meant. Fair elections and freedom of speech became an integral part of Ukrainian life.

Riding on this wave of freedom, not long after the Maidan uprising, I started working as a journalist. I quickly managed to have some success, getting ahead without the customary bribes, acquaintances or connections. When I talk about Ukraine with my Western friends, I often cite my own life story as an example of why I love this country so much. With a strong will, a thirst for knowledge and hard work, you can quickly achieve something here, getting a quality education and building an honest career—even if you grow up poor.

The excitement of the 2004 revolution had begun to fade by 2013. It was becoming obvious that the country was losing its freedom and dignity. And Viktor Yanukovych was to blame for many of our problems. The president of Ukraine imprisoned his political opponents, his entourage created corruption schemes to steal state resources and he went after independent media. The magazine where I worked, for example, was bought by an oligarch with ties to Yanukovych. The new management banned criticism of the president and his entourage, so our entire editorial staff resigned in protest. Finally, Yanukovych did not sign an association agreement with the European Union, choosing instead to ally himself with Russian President Vladimir Putin. That's when Ukrainian society exploded again, leading to another round of massive protests in Independence Square. This is how the Revolution of Dignity began in the fall of 2013.

I went to the Maidan every day that fall. For me, the protest was personal: I had worked only in independent media, where there was no censorship. Yanukovych's team, however, was destroying journalism; without freedom of the press, I simply

Olena picks up litter. Maidan, Kyiv. 2014. Photograph by Kristina Berdynskykh.

Mykola fed more than 2,400 people each day with borsch and kulish, preparing 8 big cauldrons of food daily. Maidan, Kyiv. 2014. Photograph by Kristina Berdynskykh.

could not and did not want to work. But what worried me the most was that our independent, democratic country was being pushed back into the Soviet past, deprived of its future. Ukrainians refused to put up with this, and there was nothing the government could do about it. During the Revolution of Dignity, special forces brutally beat students who gathered on the Maidan at night; the following day, hundreds of thousands of people took to the streets of Kyiv. Among them were people who had never protested before.

I went to Maidan to collect people's stories. They had come from all over Ukraine. They were young and old, they were poor and well-off. Not a single person refused to talk to me, despite the possible danger that posed to them. On the contrary, people wanted to show that they were not afraid. It was important to them. I was struck, too, by how quickly Ukrainians organized themselves. Some people made sandwiches and tea in field kitchens off the square, while others joined the Maidan self-defense, provided first aid, painted portraits, sang and gave lectures on economics. Today, during the full-scale war with Russia, some wonder how Ukrainians can raise funds to buy foreign drones in a few days. In Ukraine, this does not surprise anyone. The legacy of the Revolution of Dignity, of volunteering and organizing, remains strong.

Artists paint scenes on tents at their inhabitants' request. Maidan, Kyiv. 2014. Photograph by Kristina Berdynskykh.

When I started to document the lives of the people of Maidan, I never imagined in my worst nightmares that any of the participants would die. But it happened. One of the first people to die on the Maidan was Serhiy Nigoyan, a 20-year-old man I spoke to on January 3, 2014. And now, in 2022, it is happening again. Photographer Max Levin, who had covered the events on the Maidan, was killed by the Russian military in March 2022.

After Maidan, Russia occupied Crimea and started the war in Donbas. Yanukovych fled to Russia. No, Ukraine has not entirely overcome corruption, and its economy still needs to be reformed. But the country has dramatically changed. Ukraine is that much closer to European integration. Civil society has become far stronger, and we are led by a president—Volodymyr Zelensky—who is now an international hero.

In March 2022, Kherson, my birthplace, was occupied by Russian troops. Mykolaiv, where I studied, suffered greatly from Russian shelling. My alma mater is largely destroyed, damaged by Russian missiles. I spent the first 17 nights of the war in the Kyiv subway, hiding from the shelling. These days, I am convinced that Russia is losing the war. Putin, I believe, does not understand Ukrainians. He didn't in 2014, and he doesn't today. As for Ukrainians, we know who we are. Now more than ever. ❈

OKSANA, 22

Oksana lives in the Lviv region and studies history at university. She went to Maidan for the first time on November 25 and stayed at a hostel. On the 29th, the Berkut—the special police force—started to attack. Oksana was with some other students. "I was beaten," she says, "but others were beaten even worse. I don't want to speak about this." The only thing she'll say about that night is that while running away from the Berkut, she and some other people hid in a café until 7 a.m. and then went to St. Michael's Cathedral. She left for home on November 30 and didn't tell her parents about that night.

On December 2, although her parents were totally against it, Oksana returned to Maidan. She began to supervise one of the field kitchens. During the following month, she returned home a couple of times to sit for some exams, but afterward, she stayed in Maidan and volunteered wherever she was needed.

Since February 18, Oksana devoted her time to one thing only: helping families of the dead to organize funerals. "Somebody had to do it, so I just began to do it," she says. "I came to Maidan not to have a good time, but to help. But of course, I never imagined that I would have to help with funerals." When she bought the first coffin, she felt sick. During the first few days, she thought she was losing her mind. She had to connect with mortuaries and the prosecutors' office, organize identification of bodies and talk with families. Memorial services were held every day. Considering the emotional state of victims' relatives, volunteers tried to do everything regarding the funerals by themselves, even down to buying clothes for the dead. "Now I know that a dead person needs shoes with laces and two or three sizes bigger. I wish I didn't know it," Oksana says. Often, she didn't have to pay for clothes and shoes because salesmen gave them to her for free.

Also, volunteers had to pass aid money to the families of those killed. Some refused to accept it. "One guy's mom called and said that she didn't want any money. Instead, she asked Oksana "to show her the animal that killed her child." Oksana had no answer. Many refused to believe they had lost a loved one. "They lost their children, so their reaction was totally understandable," Oksana says, particularly as some of the dead had only arrived at Maidan the day before tragedy struck.

Oksana continues to do her work. The day she spoke to me for this story, she said, one more guy died at a hospital. He was 21. I can't imagine how such a young girl can be so strong. Oksana is a hero to me.

VOLODYMYR, 42

Volodymyr is from Sevastopol. He came to Kyiv a week and a half into the protests. "I didn't like what I saw on TV. I thought: what a horrible thing people did to Kyiv by turning it into a rubbish dump," he says. "But I came to see for myself what was actually going on here." Volodymyr was shocked by the difference between what he assumed was happening and the reality. He says that the information he got in Sevastopol was far from truthful. "Some people in Sevastopol were saying that the Banderovites [Ukrainian nationalists] would come and hang those who speak Russian," he says. Even his mother, wife and mother-in-law believed it. When he called his wife, she said he was a traitor and an enemy. His friends stopped answering his calls after he left for Maidan. "I tried to explain that I'm here not to support any politicians, not to campaign for anybody. I tried to explain what was really going on here, but nobody wanted to listen." Volodymyr's wife works at a shop and is afraid to go home alone; she is worried about her safety and that of her family because her husband is at Maidan. But he isn't ready to go home yet. Volodymyr sees that all of the people at Maidan desire peace, not war, and that's why he doesn't accept the current situation in the Crimea. He is totally against the war. "I'm a builder, not a warrior, and I want peace for my country," he says.

VALENTYNA, 49

Valentyna was born in Ukraine's Poltava region and now lives in Kyiv. She has been coming to the Euromaidan since the very first days of the protests. She reads her poetry there and also helps out in the kitchen. On the morning of January 22, Valentyna was on Hrushevskoho Street. It was quiet at first. An elderly man and woman were standing next to her. "The assault by the police began awfully quickly; we didn't understand what was going on," Valentyna says. They began to run from Hrushevskogo Street to Khreschatyk Street. Valentyna says that Berkut, the special police, knocked the old man to the ground and started brutally beating him. Valentyna was screaming and begging them to stop, but she couldn't get any closer. Boys from the Interior Troops were standing beside them. "Police officers, they're so young. I realized that they didn't like what they were witnessing, but they weren't stopping the Berkut from beating people," Valentyna says. Then she fell on her knees in front of them, but that didn't help either. Valentyna doesn't know what happened to that old man afterward.

I warned Valentyna to weigh her words carefully for this interview, because the authorities had already begun hunting for Maidan activists. "I am a political prisoner's granddaughter. My grandfather served 30 years in prison fighting this regime," she told me. "He always said, 'As long as you have your tongue, do not hold it back: speak.' So in the loving memory of my grandfather, I say what I can."

Valentyna has a grown-up daughter and a son. They work, and they help her out when it comes to chores at home. "My son cooks meals, because his mother participates in the revolution," she says smiling. I ask why she is wearing an embroidered tablecloth, and she explains that her neighbors—old women—had embroidered it with their own hands and gave it to her after they found out she was taking an active part in the events. They told her that it would protect her.

BOGDAN IVANOVYCH, 72

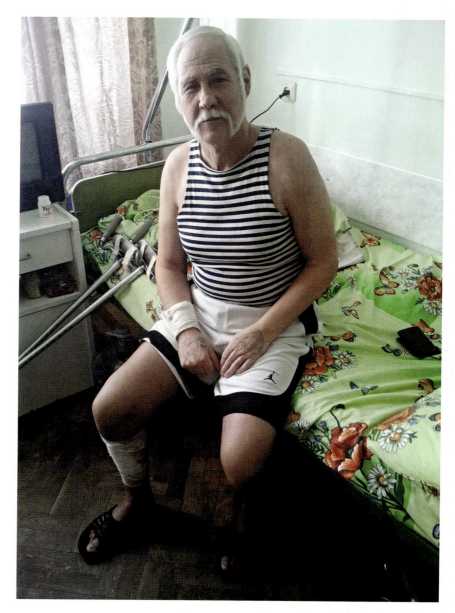

I visited Bogdan Ivanovych at a hospital in Lviv. Married with three daughters and six grandchildren (four boys and two girls), he's a very active man: he teaches computer science and informatics at a lyceum and also cares for his 92-year-old mother.

During the Maidan uprising, he was part of the 29th battalion; on the evening of January 19, he was stationed next to some buses that caught fire. The armed forces used tear gas and sound grenades, while the protesters were making their own Molotov cocktails. Ivanovych remembers how the residents on Grushevskogo street used ropes to pass milk cartons from their balconies down to the protesters.

Later on, the armed forces brought a water cannon into play, but it broke down and they had to hook it up to a water hydrant. Icy water poured down on the protesters. The outside temperature was way below freezing. Ivanovych recalls how a powerful stream of ice-cold water hit him on the chest—like being hit with a hammer, he says. He tried to ignore the feeling at first, but when he finally got back to the tent to change, he started coughing up blood. The next day, he decided to go back home and have his lungs checked out by a doctor. Afterward, he went right back to Maidan.

He got his first leg injury on February 18 during the march to the parliament, thanks to the "titushkas" who were occupying the Mariinskyi park and throwing grenades at the protesters. One of them hit Ivanovych. It wasn't a regular sound grenade, but a self-made one, stuffed with nails. "I had long underwear, a thick pair of jeans and military camouflage on," he recalls, "and all of it was ripped apart."

The surrounding action distracted his attention from the pain. He didn't feel anything. Later, he got the medical care he needed and immediately went back to the barricades. On the second day, he was running in the direction of Zhovtnevyi Palace. "I saw a sniper lying on the lawn just 50 to 70 meters away," he tells me. Someone was calling from the Maidan stage: "It's a trap!" He was moving down the left side of Instituska street and he saw how guys were dropping dead while moments before he had tried to warn them to avoid direct attack from the armed forces. He dragged away an old man who had been eager to face the attackers. Later, Ivanovych got hit by another grenade on the same leg. "It hurt, but that was irrelevant at that point," he recalls.

On the 21st, he went to seek further medical help and had to go in to have the dressing changed over the next few days. On the 25th, he went back home. He couldn't flex his leg properly anymore, so his daughter took him to the hospital. He has had a few surgeries—the last one was a skin graft. Ivanovych says he has lost his sense of taste, too, but compared to the problems with his leg, it's nothing. In any case, he is an optimist. He's sure his wounds will heal, and he says that if there is a military threat again, he'll be there to protect his Fatherland.

SOUND BITES

...between November 21, 2013 and February 22, 2014,...we experienced the essence of what it means to be human—dignity, self-sacrifice, pride, fear, sorrow, joy, communion. Collectively, we experienced a people becoming a nation.
—Mychailo Wynnyckyj, *Ukraine's Maidan, Russia's War*, 2019

"Ukraine is a country for people with very strong nerves."
—Mariya Berlinska, Head of the Ukrainian Center for Aerial Reconnaissance, aviation explorer and army volunteer, 2017

DO YOU KNOW THE UKRAINIAN NIGHT? OH, YOU DO NOT KNOW THE UKRAINIAN NIGHT! LOOK AT IT: THE MOON LOOKS OUT FROM THE CENTRE OF THE SKY.
—NIKOLAI GOGOL, EVENINGS ON A FARM NEAR DIKANKA, 1832

IN PARIS, EVERYBODY IS IN BLACK! BUT YOU KNOW, IN UKRAINE EVERYONE WEARS BRIGHT COLORS.
—OLGA KURYLENKO, UKRAINIAN-FRENCH ACTRESS, 2013

"You cannot lead Maidan, you can only join it."
—Ruslana Lyzhychko, Ukraine's 2004 Eurovision winner, 2013

The difference between a city and a person is that a city can't love you back, but Kyiv frequently gives the impression that it is trying.
—Rosa Lyster, "My Accidental Visit to the Pandemic's Party Capital," *New York Times*, 2021

Corruption is Ukraine's main enemy; we must destroy it. It's really painful to hear that Ukraine is the most corrupt country in Europe.
—Vitali Klitschko, Mayor of Kyiv, 2015

Kyiv has changed so much since the revolution that it's almost unrecognizable. I used to want to move to Europe, but Europe has come to us instead.
—Diana Lyubarskaya, actress, 2015

At this point the question of Ukraine is the most important. The situation in Ukraine is very bad. If we don't take steps now to improve the situation, we may lose Ukraine. The objective should be to transform Ukraine, in the shortest period of time, into a real fortress of the U.S.S.R.
—Joseph Stalin, 1932

IT'S A VICTORY WHEN THE WEAPONS FALL SILENT AND PEOPLE SPEAK UP.
—PRESIDENT VOLODYMYR ZELENSKY, 2019

PHOTO CREDITS: p. 4 Antonov AN-225 by Pavel Vanka (CC BY-NC-ND 2.0), medals (CC0 1.0), Bomb dismantling by Vladimir Solovyev (TASS), Tunnel of Love by Myroslava Rakovet (CC BY-SA 3.0), Don't give it to a Russian (Facebook: Не дай русскому), Wooden Church by Elena Kurylo (CC BY-SA 4.0), World's largest crossword by Ivanko1 (CC0 1.0), p. 5 Comfort Town by ver0nicka/Shutterstock, Millionaires Ghost Town by krblokhin/iStock, Human skin gloves by Voytikof (CC BY-SA 4.0), balaclava by Tobias "ToMar" Maier (CC BY-SA 3.0), Trembita by mik Krakow (CC BY-NC-ND 2.0), Pop-up synagogue by REUTERS/Gleb Garanich, Vitaly Klitschko by Vuxicon MediaEmp (CC BY-ND 2.0), Little green men by photo.ua/Shutterstock, Dmitry Khaladzhi (Instagram: dmitriykhaladzhi), Red Forest Chernobyl by Frode Bjorshol (CC BY 2.0), p. 33 Pysanka Easter Egg by nejix (CC BY-NC-SA 2.0) Museum of Sexual Cultures by Zolotorev Pavel (CC0 1.0), Lenins in sunglasses by Kryvosheia Yurii/Shutterstock, Miniature ship by Eddie Gerald/Alamy Stock Photo, p. 37 Spotykac by TravelingOtter (CC BY-SA 2.0), Peasant blouse by A. M. Bulk (CC BY 2.0), Musician by Oli Zitch (CC BY-NC-ND 2.0), Rave by A_Lesik/Shutterstock, Rainbow arch by vvoe/Shutterstock, Iceland by Tien 3ashien (Still of YouTube video), p. 42 Yanukovych & Putin by Premier.gov.ru (CC BY 4.0), Maidan by Sasha Maksymenko (CC BY 2.0), Separatists by Deni Kornilov/Shutterstock, Lenin on a crane by Yurchyks/Shutterstock, p. 43 Maidan protests by Sasha Maksymenko (CC BY 2.0), old Ukrainian flag by Zscout370 (CC0 1.0), Servant of the People (fair use), p. 66 Map of languages by DiscoverWithDima (CC BY-SA 4.0), p. 77 Bessarabska Square Lenin by Efrem Lukatsky/Associated Press, Darth Vader Lenin (Twitter screenshot), Lenin in garbage by rootstocks/iStock, p. 78 Kryjivka by Adam Jones (CC BY 2.0), p. 81 Petro Oliynik in Honka by Darmon Richter, p. 100 Altar (Instagram screenshot) #HexPutin (Medium screenshot), sigil (Instagram screenshot), ceremony (Instagram screenshot), p. 103 Amusement park by Henrik Ismarker (CC BY-NC-ND 2.0), Baba Hana by Ma White (CC BY-NC 2.0), Church of St. Elias by Eamonn Butler (CC BY 2.0), Chernobyl coffee by Omri Westmark (CC BY 2.0), Przewalski's horses by Michael Kötter (CC BY-NC-SA 2.0), p. 114 Nina Petrovna Khrushcheva by Zeinab Mohamed (CC BY-NC-SA 2.0), Leon Trotsky (CC0 1.0), Sergei Korolev by Album/Alamy Stock Photo, Nikolay Gogol by Tretyakov Gallery (CC0 1.0), Leonid Zhabotinsky by Unknown (Svenska Pressfoto) (CC0 1.0), Vera Kholodnaya by Unknown (CC0 1.0), Yakov Smirnoff by peachsmack (CC BY-SA 2.0), p. 11 Flag by New Africa/Shutterstock, Bread stamp by Укрпошта (CC0 1.0), Korovai by AMartiniouk (CC BY-SA 3.0), p. 124-7 First-person portraits by Kristina Berdynskykh